THE FRENCH FOREIGN LEGION

The French Foreign Legion is shrouded in mystery and has cultivated a fearsome reputation - envied by its allies. It is one of the last military formations in the world that recruits on reputation, refusing to engage with any marketing campaign. Each day, Legion hopefuls arrive in France to join up, with an average of 9,000 hoping to be accepted each year – an average of just 1,100 are. This elite force emerged in the 1800s, formed from refugees in France. Its ethos of never surrender was forged at Camerone in Mexico when a handful of legionnaires fought to the death against more than 2,000 Mexican soldiers. The Legion offers men from all over the world a fresh start in life with a new identity. Some arrive after a period in prison, others simply run away from domestic issues. It is professional military force, contributing to French national defence and in recent years has deployed on operations to the Congo, Burkina Faso, Mali, Lebanon, and Afghanistan.

Instantly recognised for their distinctive white kepis and green and red epaulettes, the regiment marches at a slow pace – often supported by a marching song. After assessment in Paris or Aubange those selected are sent to Castelnaudary in southern France to begin training and four months of intense infantry tactics to shape them into Legionnaires. The coveted white kepi is presented after a final endurance march in the Pyrenees which sees the recruits accepted into the regiment. From here they will go to serve with one of the Legion's units and specialise as paratroopers, radio operators or engineers. Within two years most will be deployed on operations.

Newly qualified recruits parade wearing the white kepi and traditional red epaulettes. Soldiers wear a black chin strap while corporals have gold straps. (Andy Darby/DPL)

CONTENTS

03 Welcome
Shrouded in mystery, the French Foreign Legion has cultivated a fearsome reputation - envied by its allies. It is one of the last military formations in the world that recruits on reputation. Each day Legion hopefuls arrive in France to join up, with an average of 9,000 hoping to be accepted. Its ethos of never surrender was forged in 1863 at Camerone in Mexico when a handful of legionnaires fought to the death against more than 2,000 Mexican soldiers.

06 Joining the French Foreign Legion
A career in the French Foreign Legion is not for the faint-hearted. The regiment ignores the post-modern world of woke and social correctness. It is unapologetic about any alleged combat indiscretions during its colonial past and instead, it celebrates its military traditions with regimental pride and songs. This is a unique force that defies convention and as most countries in the West currently face recruiting challenges in the 21st century, the Legion faces an overload of applicants.

18 The Sacred Artifact – Captain Danjou's Wooden Hand
The Legion's most holy artifact represents the regiment's defiant philosophy that bonds every man in an oath of 'never surrender'. No matter what the threat, this extreme mantra is simple; soldiers may die in combat, regiments can be destroyed in battle, but the Legion always lives on. This pledge of brotherhood is best explained by the actions of Captain Jean Danjou in 1863 at the Battle of Camerone in Mexico.

30 The Training begins – March or Die
The Legion's training barracks are located on the outskirts of Castelnaudary, a country town in southern France, sometimes referred to by recruits as 'Castel'. Only recruits who have passed all the extra assessments, criminal checks, psychometric tests, and medicals at Aubagne will make their way to Toulouse. With new identities now confirmed, clothing and equipment issued, and contracts signed these recruits are members of the Legion.

42 The Expendables – Legion History
The French Foreign Legion has a unique approach to combat which has shaped the regiment's ethos into a sacred order of fighting men. They prefer death to dishonour and in battle these soldiers accept that they expendable in the name of the Legion. From famous battles to its passionate music and marching songs, the Legion has 'cult status' in which recruits accept the indoctrination into this regiment of strangers, or they quickly leave.

54 New World Conflicts
Algeria is the spiritual home of the French Foreign Legion. For decades Paris deployed legionnaires here where they trained and stood at readiness to defend the colonial empire. The north African country had been under French control since the 1830s and after World War Two France sought to maintain its cultural grip and control of sovereignty. But a growing number of Algerians wanted independence. In May 1945 demonstrations demanding self- rule took place across the country.

66 Out of Area Operations
Since its formation, the Legion has been deployed overseas protecting the country's interests and when required fighting for France. The departure from north Africa forced changes and new deployments for the Legion to overseas territories, in Madagascar and then in Guiana, Djibouti, French Polynesia, and the archipelago of the Comoros Islands.

78 The Gulf War and Operations in Africa
The start of the 1990s saw conflict in the Gulf, and the collapse of the Soviet Union in December 1991 generated a flood of recruits to the Legion from eastern Europe, changing the composition of the regiment for the next decade. At the same time the end of the Cold War had acted as a catalyst for conflict in regions where Moscow had been politically dominant.

92 The REP – The Legion's Paratroopers
The Legion's elite unit is the 2nd Foreign Parachute Regiment, often referred to simply as the REP. It is the regiment's only airborne unit and delivers the special operations capability to move anywhere at short notice. After France agreed to Algerian independence the REP moved to Corsica in 1967 and from here it has been regularly sent on operations across the globe.

104 New Wars – Afghanistan and into Mali
In the 21st century the pace of operational commitment has not slowed for the French Foreign Legion. As new wars emerged in an era of Islamic terrorism the Legion spent a decade in Afghanistan fighting the Taliban as part of an international coalition and then moved into Mali, the former French colony, after a request was made to Paris for assistance.

Ranks of the French Foreign Legion shown alongside their UK and US Army equivalents

Legion	British Army	US Army
Legionnaire	Private	E1 Private
Caporal	Corporal	Corporal
Caporal-chef*	Senior Corporal (unique rank)	None
Sergent	Sergeant (UK)	Gunnery Sergeant
Sergent-chef*	Colour Sergeant (UK)	Master Sergeant (US)
Adjudant	Warrant Officer 2	Warrant officer (Class Two)
Adjudant-chef*	Warrant Officer 1	Chief Warrant Officer
Aspirant	Officer Cadet	Cadet
Sous Lieutenant	2nd Lieutenant	2nd Lieutenant
Lieutenant	Lieutenant	Lieutenant
Capitaine	Captain	Captain
Major	Major	Major
Lieutenant-Colonel	Lieutenant Colonel	Lieutenant Colonel
Colonel	Colonel	Colonel
Commandant	Brigadier	Brigadier General

* The rank of caporal chef is an appointment rather than a rank, often given to a very senior, experienced legionnaire. If a caporal chef wants to be promoted to sergent (sergeant) he must go back to legionnaire and be officially promoted to corporal. To complicate matters, the use of the word 'chef' in the ranks of sergent and adjudant signifies that they are senior in experience and rank and can proceed up the promotion chain.

ISBN: 9781802829655
Editor: David Reynolds
Senior editor, specials: Roger Mortimer
Email: roger.mortimer@keypublishing.com
Cover Design: Steve Donovan
Design: SJmagic DESIGN SERVICES, India
Advertising Sales Manager: Sam Clark
Email: sam.clark@keypublishing.com
Tel: 01780 755131
Advertising Production: Becky Antoniades
Email: Rebecca.antoniades@keypublishing.com

SUBSCRIPTION/MAIL ORDER
Key Publishing Ltd, PO Box 300, Stamford, Lincs, PE9 1NA
Tel: 01780 480404
Subscriptions email: subs@keypublishing.com
Mail Order email: orders@keypublishing.com
Website: www.keypublishing.com/shop

PUBLISHING
Group CEO and Publisher: Adrian Cox

Published by
Key Publishing Ltd, PO Box 100, Stamford, Lincs, PE9 1XQ
Tel: 01780 755131
Website: www.keypublishing.com

PRINTING
Precision Colour Printing Ltd, Haldane, Halesfield 1, Telford, Shropshire. TF7 4QQ

DISTRIBUTION
Seymour Distribution Ltd, 2 Poultry Avenue, London, EC1A 9PU

Enquiries Line: 02074 294000.

THE ARMY OF CHOICE

Joining the French Foreign Legion

A French Foreign Legion soldier in his ceremonial dress. This is what thousands of young men aspire to be. (Yves Debay/DPL)

In many ways, the French Foreign Legion is a regiment apart from others. It pays scant regard to political correctness that many western armies have embraced. It ignores the post-modern world of woke and social correctness and is unapologetic about any alleged combat indiscretions during its colonial past in Indochina and Algeria. Instead, it celebrates its military traditions with regimental pride and marching songs. This is a force that defines itself by its discipline and does not suffer problems with 'medical non-deployable' soldiers that have hampered UK and US forces. Critically, while most armies in the West face recruiting challenges in the 21st century, the Legion has no such problem. In 2022, the UK Ministry of Defence spent £70 million on recruiting, while the United States military invested $314 million, both forces continue to face personnel challenges. The Legion has no recruiting campaign, offers no incentives or encouragement, yet it routinely attracts in excess of 9,000 hopeful candidates every year who aspire to join - of which just 1,200 make it through the training. In fact, those who seek to join the Legion trek from far and wide, arriving from Brazil, the United States, Canada, the UK, Germany, Poland, Italy, Romania, and the Baltic States - at their own expense.

The regiment's culture is based on a maxim that the Legion is your family. Those who join require a strong mental attitude and understanding that an individual must put the regiment above anything else. In Legion parlance, there is nothing else – the Legion is your fatherland (Legio Patria Nostra). It has a global reputation which for generations has drawn men seeking adventure. Many see it as a sanctuary to escape their past, having committed heinous crimes, some simply want to become Legionnaires, while others seek to escape failed marriages or a life that is consumed by routine. But 'ordinary' is not in the Legion's vernacular, this is a brotherhood which bonds men of all races and creeds from Christians to Jews, Muslims, and Buddhists. Volunteers from China, South America and increasingly the United States and Britain see the Legion as a second chance at life. The British often group together and are known as the 'anglais

The Legion refuses to advertise and instead relies on stories such as 'Beau Geste' to encourage recruits from around the world to join. (Paul Dupont/FFL)

The vision of the French Foreign Legion as a force which is always in action has helped generate a mythical impression of the regiment. (Yves Debay/DPL)

During World War Two, the British commander Field Marshal Viscount Alanbrooke wrote that he was impressed with the Legion, saying they looked like of body of lean hard men. (DPL archives)

Men from all races and religious divides must work together and put aside any differences. (Australian MoD)

mafia' – the British mafia. If a Ukrainian and Russian recruit find themselves in the same section, they must treat each other as brothers and forget any national disputes.

While the Legion guards its ranks as a 'men only' force, the French government allows women to serve in the regiment, but they are not allowed to take part in the four-month infantry course and are prevented from wearing the coveted white kepi. One notable exception was made during World War Two when British nurse Susan Travers served with the French

The majority of applicants head for Paris, travelling into Charles de Gaulle airport or by train arriving at Gare du Nord. (TGV)

Red Cross in the Italian campaign and on the Western Front. After the war she applied and was formally enrolled into the Legion Estrangere as an adjutant-chef and later married Legion Adjutant Chef Nicolas Schlegelmilch. Men between the ages of 17 and 40, of any nationality, may join the legion.

Recruits enlist under an assumed name—a requirement known as the anonymat—but a legionnaire may request to serve under his true name after a year of service. Although the regiment shields every legionnaire's privacy, each prospective recruit is thoroughly interrogated to discover his motivation for joining and to determine whether he has a criminal background. Those who have had minor scrapes with the law are acceptable, but today the legion is more selective about who it takes than it was during its early history.

The decision to join the French Foreign Legion needs careful consideration, it is physically tough and psychologically intense. It is a career choice for those seeking a new life, for some an adventure and for others an opportunity to test themselves. Men do not join for the money; they sign up for the spirit of being a Legionnaire. Those who pass will accept the code of honour and the belief that their brotherhood is immortal on the battlefield and that the regiment can never be killed. Legion training carves young men into tough individuals capable of coping with almost any situation in which they find themselves. They thrive on wearing the beret and badge, proud, exceptional, and full of self-confidence.

Recruits enlist under an assumed identity, and after a year a legionnaire may request to serve under his true name. (DPL)

It is common for applicants to be anxious when they arrive in Paris. Many have second thoughts, some stop and get back on the train, others enjoy a final coffee or something stronger. (Paris TB)

At Fort de Nogent the guard will ask to see your passport and having checked it will ask if you are ready to give up everything and sign away five years of your life. (FFL)

During World War Two, the British commander Field Marshal Viscount Alanbrooke witnessed the Legion in North Africa and commented on their presence, he said : "Out of the fast-failing light and through the failing snow flakes came a sight I shall never forget. The grandest assembly of real fighting men that I have ever seen, marching with their heads up as if they owned the world, lean, hard looking men, carrying their arms admirably and marching with perfect precision."

Those who join the French Foreign Legion must be sure that this is the life they aspire to. Life in the Legion is a life-changing decision. Once you have completed training you will serve in one of the Legion's elite regiments and join a force stationed in France, Djibouti, Corsica, or South America. To enlist you must obtain a visa and travel to France making sure you have an official form of identity on you, such as a passport or driving licence. The Legion does not accept online applications or letters – you must attend in person. Once in France, potential recruits can head for regional recruiting offices in Paris at Fort de Nogent, or Lille, Nantes, Strasbourg, Bordeaux, Lyon,

On arrival in Marseille some rookies go into the town again for a final meal and drink. (Marseille Council)

Above the entrance of the fort are the words 'Legion Etrangere'. There is no set routine or protocol here, men just arrive, and knock on the wooden door. (FFL)

Bastille Day offers the chance to see the Legion up close as they take part in the annual parade. (FFL)

Perpignan, or Toulouse. Here applicants will be processed and given a rail fare to the Legion's headquarters at Aubagne. Recruits will face a physical assessment, confirmation that they can read and write in their own language as well as a medical and dental check.

Aspiring legionnaires are advised to take minimum clothing which should include running shoes, T-shirts, and shorts as well as basic toiletries. Any valuables such as expensive cameras and laptops should be left behind and it is advisable to wear casual clothes. If you arrive in a suit, you will stand out and bring attention to yourself. If you do not speak French, it is advisable to buy a phrase book which will be useful to get you through the journey and help you on the course, being able to speak the language is critical. The majority of applicants head for Paris, travelling into Charles de Gaulle airport or by train arriving at Gare du Nord, then picking up the Paris Metro to the nearest Metro station at Val de Fontenay station or by bus to Maurice Couderchet or Nogent Sur Mare.

It is common for applicants to be anxious when they arrive in Paris. Many have second thoughts, some stop and get back on the train, others enjoy a final coffee or something stronger. The final approach to the fort involves passing through a housing complex and the Impasse de la Croix Pommier – at the end of the road the fort is in sight. It is imposing, a huge stone wall on the left and an arched entranced with the words 'Legion Etrangerere' above it. There is no set routine or protocol here, men just arrive, walk through the arch, and knock on the wooden door of what appears to be a guardroom.

Inside the fort in Paris the grounds are kept in immaculate condition. (FFL)

Bastille Day in Paris often attracts budding legionnaires who want to see the Legion before they join. (FFL)

Recruits who report to the fort or direct to Aubagne will be given presentations about the training ahead of them and what to expect. (Yves Debay /DPL)

Some decide this is the time to turn around and leave. The guard will ask to see your passport and having checked it he will ask if you are ready to give up everything and sign away five years of your life. Applicants are then escorted up a set of stairs to a room where other hopefuls are often sat waiting. For the Legion the daily arrival of new blood is routine, and the staff are in no rush – sometimes rookies sit for hours waiting to be interviewed. On average, 40 applications are made to the Legion every day, many are declined, mainly on medical grounds, with only a small percentage being accepted for training.

There will be some volunteers who have military experience, others who have absolutely no idea what they are signing up for, and those who after a few days realise that this is not for them. Nationalities always gravitate towards each other. There are periods when the number of volunteers from Britain and America spike, most often when the two countries are not involved in conflicts or major operations such as Iraq and Afghanistan. In 2015, a year after the end of UK combat operations in Helmand, southern Afghanistan, the Legion saw a small lift in applications from the UK. One of them, Dean had done well at school, but said his world fell apart when he failed to be selected for officer training at the British Army's Sandhurst academy. He was convinced it was because his face did not fit with the 'university class' recruited by Sandhurst. Frustrated and angry, he travelled to France and made his way to Fort Nugent. He recounted his anxiety of arriving

Those recruits the instructors think are suitable will be called into the office and given a rail fare and told to take the train from Gare du Nord to Marseille in the south of France. (TGV)

at the base, saying: "I wasn't sure that this was what I wanted, but I needed to prove to myself that I had ability. Fort Nugent was bleak, maybe not helped by the fact that it was a freezing January day when I arrived. The corporal chef looked up and ushered me to follow him into what appeared to be a waiting room and said, 'sit here Johnny'. I later discovered that all English are dubbed 'Johnny' or 'roast beef'. I met five others on that first day, two Polish lads, a Latvian, an Irish lad and a Canadian. We were told to line up in a corridor and in turn we faced what they called the chocolate bar – a metal pole positioned 6ft high across the corridor – which we had to jump up to catch and perform as many pull-ups as we could, we were then escorted to a cook house and later escorted to a room full of bunk beds. No sheets just blankets. The following day we were asked about criminal convictions and questioned yet again about why we wanted to join the Legion."

Those recruits the instructors think are suitable will be called into the office and given a rail fare and told to take the train from Gare du Nord to Marseille in the south of France. It takes about four hours and passes through spectacular countryside. If you have a translation book, now is the time to read it. At Aubagne there is little patience for those who do not speak French. Before you arrive in France the most important requirement, after making sure you are super fit, is to learn as much of the language as you can. It will make life much easier. On arrival in Marseille some rookies go into the town again for a final meal and drink at the surprisingly named Red Lion pub, perhaps a last phone call home and some final thinking to convince themselves they are doing the right thing. Some will have chosen to report directly to Aubagne and arrive at the main gate their hearts pumping with anxiety and fear about what is to ahead of them.

Among the presentations give to the budding recruits will be a list of career opportunities to serve as snipers and radio operators. (FFL)

There are several ways to get to the base; some get a bus; others share a taxi along the A50 to Aubagne. Here the legionnaire on the main gate will also ask new arrivals if they are 'sure' they want to join. Once inside the rookies are marched to a room, where they receive a brief about what will happen that day. Then they are taken to the clothing store and issued with a track suit, it bears a small legion motif and ensures that staff across the base can instantly identify new recruits. The next visit is to the barbers for a 'shaven head'. Mark, from Liverpool, joined the Legion in 2007 and deserted a year after he left training. He said he remembers being in the queue and seeing all the shaven heads ahead of him. He added: "Most of them had cuts and scars on their heads. We had a Romanian cage fighter who had previously earned a living fighting anyone that his gang boss told him to, so he ran off to join the legion. His head was covered in scars."

Marseille has close links with the Legion and celebrates Bastille Day every year with a parade headed by the regiment. (FFL)

Within a couple of hours of arriving at Aubagne the budding legionnaires will make a declaration and sign a contract to the legion. This is it, once the paperwork is signed recruits are in the legion. More checks will take place here, particularly the 'gestapo' test in which recruits are asked more questions about their background to ensure they are not being chased by the police. Educational background will not matter, neither will your status, religion, race, or the fact that on arrival you cannot speak French.

In the first week individuals face intense physical and medical assessment. Volunteers must pass a bleep test, swim 25 metres and complete a series of pull-ups. The medical and dental check is vigorous with the maximum number of missing teeth allowed being four. Doctors will also check for diabetes, hepatitis, cancer, hernias, as well as any mental health issues. Finally, tattoos are allowed with the exception of Nazi emblems and any marks on the face. At Aubagne recruits will be required to learn about the regiment's traditions, its ceremonial protocols and ethos. The medics aim to 'weed-out' those with mental health problems, but there are always a few who slip through the net for the instructors to identify and dismiss during their first few days at Aubagne.

The Legion moved to France from its Algerian barracks at Sidi-bel-Abbès, after the north African country won independence from Paris. The French Army decided that for the first time in its history, the Legion would have its headquarters in mainland France. The regiment quickly adapted and accepted the move to Aubagne, a German naval base during World War Two, and moved forward. Today, the base maintains the same principles as it always has – every man has a chance to prove himself and once the contract is signed the Legion owns you. It is possible to leave in some extreme cases, but these are rare – once signed you belong to the Legion for five years. It is often at the point of signing that some men suddenly realise the commitment they have signed up for and leave the only way they

Inside the base at Aubagne, the headquarters of the Legion, sits the monument to the dead. (FFL)

At Aubagne recruits will see trained legionnaires marching around the base wearing the white Kepi. (Yves Debay/DPL)

Most tattoos such as this are accepted, but facial marks or any Nazi insignia will result in a would-be legionnaire being turned away. (Julie Agnes)

At Aubagne recruits are likely to encounter regimental buglers, often a caporal chef on parade. (FFL)

Images of the Legion on operations adorn the walls of the recruits' selection area at Aubagne. (FFL)

can – by deserting. Running away from the Legion is seen as cowardly and if detained the individual will face a prison term. Many young African and Arab men are physically fit, but often they fail the selection process because they cannot read or write or have a medical condition that excludes them from service.

At Aubagne, instructors waste no time in conditioning the new recruits to the Legion. As they wait to be sent to Castelnaudary and for their orders they are given cleaning tasks around the immaculate base. As the training gets underway, recruits are assigned to sections – which are 40 strong compared to just eight in the British Army. A sergeant or corporal will shape the recruits into a team at Aubagne and prepared them for the fast pace of training at Castelnaudary. The volunteers themselves have one goal to earn the right to wear the coveted white kepi – the regimental hallmark of a legionnaire. The base at Castelnaudary, the Legion's training centre, sits on the edge of a small agricultural market town about 15 miles from Toulouse. At the training base recruits are tested from the minute they arrive, and they must quickly understand that any order must be carried out instantly.

From Aubagne the recruits, not signed into the Legion, will be given a final brief and watch their instructors salute the flag before heading off. (FFL)

The days spent at Aubagne will start at 5am with physical training, a light breakfast, room, and equipment inspections, followed by a run. Here they also learn the story of Captain Danjou, an officer who was killed at the Battle of Camerone in 1863. His actions and that of his men are held as an example of the ethos of the Legion. Danjou and his legionnaires fought off thousands of Mexicans and pledged an oath to fight to the death, rather than surrender. It was their personal salute to the Legion. The officer had lost a hand during fighting in the Crimea and wore a wooden prosthetic. After the battle it was recovered and eventually passed to the regiment. Today, it is the most sacred artefact in the ceremonial room at Aubagne.

On the walls around the shrine to Capt Danjou are the names of every legionnaire who has been killed in action since its formation in 1861. This is where recruits meet the commandant of the Legion for the first time and are briefed about the regiment's history. For a legionnaire to not know and fully understand the story of Danjou is regarded as an insult to the regiment. They must know what Camerone day is about, and why it is so important, and they must understand what makes legionnaires different from the rest of the French army. After a short-time recruits move onto to Castelnaudary, where the main infantry training commences. ●

Recruits bound for Castelnaudary will catch the train from Marseille station to Toulouse. (French Railways)

CAPTAIN DANJOU'S HAND

The sacred artefact that bonds every Legionnaire

The Legion's most holy artefact represents the regiment's defiant philosophy that bonds every man in an oath of never surrender. No matter what the threat this extreme mantra of the French Foreign Legion's ethos is simple; soldiers may die in combat, regiments can be destroyed in battle, but the Legion always lives on. This pledge of brotherhood is best explained by the actions of Captain Jean Danjou in 1863 at the Battle of Camerone in Mexico. Here Danjou and his men were trying to protect a supply column when they were attacked by a 2,000 strong force of Mexican cavalry. He knew that his small unit of just 62 legionnaires could not defeat the huge force, they simply did not have enough ammunition. But he and his men vowed in the name of Legion, to fight on and not surrender.

Danjou had lost a hand when his musket exploded at the Siege of Sevastopol during the Crimean War. However, while he still had his sword hand to fight with, he had

Camerone Day is marked by all regiments of the Legion every year on April 30, and always in perfect formation. (FFL)

A model showing the uniform that a legionnaire would have worn in Mexico and the lightweight backpack compared to today's soldiers. (FFL)

A painting of Captain Danjou in his blue Legion uniform. (FFL)

equipped himself with a wooden prosthetic hand, strapped to his wrist with a large leather cuff and sheathed in a formal white glove. As they faced overwhelming odds, the remaining soldiers vowed to fight to the end. The captain was killed as were most of his men as they fought on rather than agree to surrender. The courage of Danjou and his men has become legend and is held as the ultimate example of the Legion's fighting spirit - his story is known by every man who wears the white kepi.

The French intervention in Mexico, initially supported by Britain and Spain, was mounted in July 1861 after Mexican President Benito Juárez's failure to repay loans which were due to French, British, and Spanish creditors. In 1862, French Emperor Napoleon III stated that France only wanted the debt paying and nothing else. However, behind the scenes the Emperor wanted to take advantage of the American Civil War and expand his empire in Latin-America and eventually install Maximilian of Habsburg, Archduke of Austria, as Emperor of Mexico. Both the UK and Spain saw the folly of this expedition and pulled out of the intervention. A French force sailed in early 1862 with General Elie Frederic Forey appointed commander in chief. In the letter instructing him, Emperor Napoleon had said : "There will be people who will ask why we waste so many men, and spend so much money, in establishing a regular government in Mexico. Mexico, thus regenerated, will ever be favourable to us, not only from gratitude, but also because its interests will coincide with ours, and because it will find a support in its relations with European powers." In early 1863 the French Foreign Legion regiment were sent to Mexico to reinforce the French Army and given the mission of ensuring the security of the supply convoys for the units leading the siege.

Empire Ambition

It was a plan that many advised against and in addition to the logistical challenge of mounting a military campaign in Mexico, it was clear to observers that the United States would never tolerate a European nation ruling part of the Western Hemisphere. The French Army had fought Mexican forces at Puebla, east of Mexico City, and constantly required supplies to sustain its campaign. Ammunition and food came from

The inscription on the house where Danjou was born on April 15, 1828, pays respects to his life and service. (Jules Rhin)

A celebration in front of the birthplace of Captain Danjou in Chalabre takes place every year. (Philippe Vidal)

its naval beachhead at Veracruz, where warships would arrive with stores which were offloaded and ferried by convoys of mules to the garrison. They travelled along the 250 kilometres route of isolated roads and tracks through tropical rainforests and arid open terrain. The Legion deployed units at vulnerable 'choke- points' to counter any attacks, but rarely had enough men to cover the entire route. The soldiers carried back packs with a rolled blanket, cleaning equipment for their rifles, and a small amount of food. Additional supplies were often purchased from local villages.

Their task was to defend the column at all costs, as in addition to supplies, they often carried gold to be used by the French to influence local dignitaries. The terrain hindered progress to just eight or ten miles per day and while the legionnaires slept in the countryside, the Mexican cavalry sheltered at settlements along the route. The isolated Legion patrols waited in the blistering heat for the convoy or 'caravan' as the French called it, to pass safely. These columns were often several miles long and consisted of more than 150 mules laden with equipment, ammunition, and guns. Camped in the countryside for months, legionnaires were exposed to dysentery and malaria, as well as the terrifying disease called black vomit, now more commonly known as yellow fever.

Towards the end of April 1863 an informer, paid by the French, told Legion commander Colonel Pierre Jeanningros that the next convoy would be ambushed by a large Mexican force. The procession of mules was unusually large and very special. As well as the routine loads of food and ammunition it included four million francs in gold. Protection was vital, but the Legion was short of men due to illness and Jeanningros

A painting of the battle at Camerone, where almost all the legionnaires were killed in a fight with Mexican forces. (FFL Museum)

Legionnaires at Aubagne take part in the Camerone celebrations every year. (FFL)

had few troops of his own to allocate. In addition to the convoy's small escort, he could spare only a single company, the 3rd Company of the Legion's 2nd battalion, already down to half strength. But the colonel elected to send the experienced Captain Jean Danjou as its commander. The captain would have two other officers to help him, both second lieutenants. One, Jean Napoleon Vilain, had quickly been promoted; the other, Clement Maudet, was an old sweat who had risen through the ranks to sergeant-major before winning his commission.

The French Legion commander Colonel Pierre Jeanningros was told that the next convoy would be ambushed by a large Mexican force. (FFL)

Danjou force's consisted of just 62 men and included Belgians, Swiss, Germans, Frenchmen, Poles, Dutch, and Danes. It was a typical Legion company, fiercely loyal to the regiment, its officers, and each other. But Danjou, one of the most senior captains serving with the Legion in Mexico knew he faced a huge challenge.

Camerone

Shortly after midnight on April 30, he set off with his soldiers to escort the convoy, passing through a series of small villages and hamlets. The company passed through Camarone, a small, quiet village which appeared unkempt and poor. Danjou had opted to move through Camerone and find a position where they could shelter.

He was unaware that the Mexican cavalry had been shadowing him and his soldiers, perhaps tipped off by local people. It was still dark when the legionnaires stopped to refill their water bottles at a small river on the outskirts of the village. There were a few buildings nearby and Danjou's plan was to rest and move out at 'first light'. Suddenly they were fired on from a nearby property, which was later identified as the Hacienda La Trinidad. A legionnaire was wounded in the initial engagement, which had taken the soldiers by surprise. As they scanned the area for the gunman, Danjou spotted hundreds of Mexican cavalrymen heading towards them. He ordered his men to form a hollow square – a military formation in which soldiers can fire from all four sides and designed for use against cavalry. As the Mexicans charged, the legionnaires fired volleys which broke the assault, but the captain knew the enemy was far too strong for his men to take on in the open ground and he ordered them to pull back into the village, hoping to find cover. This tiny hamlet, named after a type of shrimp, found in a nearby river, suddenly became the focus of what would become an historic battle.

The wooden hand of Captain Danjou is regarded as a sacred artefact and kept at the barracks in Aubagne. (FFL)

A drawing of events on April 30, 1863, at Camerone. (FFL Museum)

Legionnaires of the Parachute Regiment (REP) march to commemorate Camerone Day. (FFL)

The legionnaires took shelter in a stable building next to the run-down hacienda, which was surrounded by a 10-foot wall. The main building nearby was already occupied by several hundred Mexican troops. Danjou posted his men at windows and walls in the stable enclosure and had his troops use rocks and rubble to plug doorways and breaches in the walls.

They then prepared for a siege. Danjou's small force included several men with combat experience and character including Corporal Evariste Berg, an ex-officer, who had been dismissed from the regular French army for misconduct. Louis Maine, a veteran of the Crimean fighting who had given up his sergeant's stripes to enlist in the Legion, and Sergeant Vincent Morzycki a veteran of the Italian military.

The legionnaires soon started to take casualties and the situation deteriorated when their pack mules bolted at the first sound of gunfire. They carried the reserve ammunition, and the soldiers were now left with just 60 cartridges each. To add to the nightmare their extra water supplies had been on the mules and each man's personal rations were now running low. As dawn broke the number of wounded caused

Lieutenant Jean Napoleon Vilain, a member of the 3rd Company. He had been the paymaster but volunteered to deploy. (FFL)

The fighting spirit and ethos that was demonstrated by Danjou and is men is carried by today's legionnaires. (FFL)

Captain Danjou lost his hand when his musket exploded during fighting in Sevastopol. (FFL)

Danjou concern. Then at 9.30am, the Mexican commander sent a runner forward with a flag to offer the legionnaires a truce and allow them to surrender. The offer was instantly dismissed, and the runner told in colourful language to go away as the soldiers refused to consider defeat. The Mexicans later reported that they were shocked at the legionnaires response and admitted they had to respect their position.

Every Bullet Counts

The legionnaires' disciplined rifle fire, instilled in them to not to waste ammunition and make every shot count, was now vital. They inflicted heavy losses on the Mexicans, but it was now clear to Danjou that he and his men had little chance of surviving. During a lull in the fire-fight he ordered his batman to take out a bottle of wine, which he always carried for his officer. Each man was given a sip of wine and asked to make a solemn oath to the Legion not to surrender. He then raised his cup and proclaimed :"Legionnaires die better than any men in the world."

At noon on April 30, almost 12 hours after the battle had started Danjou was shot in the chest by a sniper and died. He and his brothers in arms had been totally outnumbered, yet they still fought on. Lieutenant Vilain took command of the 40 remaining men and fought on. The Mexicans offered another chance to the legionnaires to surrender, but still they declined. For a short while at noon, there had been a flash of hope. The soldiers heard drums in the distance, along with bugles, and the surviving members of Danjou's company were convinced that a French relief column was about to reinforce them. But in fact, the music and drums were additional Mexican troops. Within an hour another 1,000 Mexican infantry surrounded them. But still the surviving legionnaires refused to surrender. With no water or food, they fought on in the intense heat. Almost all the legionnaires still alive were now wounded and as Lt Vilain ran across open ground area to check on a wounded legionnaire he was shot and died. Maudet, the former sergeant major, took command of the little band that remained. The barrels of their long Le Gras rifles were far too hot to touch as the men took any ammunition they could from their dead colleagues to stay in the fight. The morning heat was nearly unbearable; the wounded were in agony, and one by one the survivors were dying. The soldiers allowed the Mexicans to advance and then hit them at close range, killing the front rank of the advancing enemy and forcing those in the rear to run for their lives. Their rifle fire held back the attackers, but time was running out. Legionnaire Maine later recalled his experience of the hellish conditions at Camerone, stating: "The heat pressed on us; the sun struck from the white walls of the courtyard, searing our eyes. When we opened our mouths to breathe, we seemed to inhale fire."

At last, nearly all the blue-coated soldiers lay still in the dirt. Only five remained standing—

The father of the regiment, Paul Frederick Rollet. (FFL)

A veteran can be seen carrying Danjou's hand at the Camerone Day parade at Aubagne. (FFL)

The Pioneer Regiment with their hallmark axes march on Camerone Day. (FFL)

Camerone Day is all about marking the exploits of the legionnaires who fought in Mexico. (FFL)

the tough Maudet, Corporal Maine, and three privates. These five surviving legionnaires were all down to their very last bullet and opted to fix bayonets and charge the enemy. In admiration of their courage the Mexican commander ordered his troops to cease fire and took them prisoner – allowing them to form an honour guard for the body of Captain Danjou.

The battle at Camerone ended after 16 hours of fighting – six of them in the blazing sunshine, during which the legionnaires had fired their entire stock of ammunition and left more than 300 Mexican soldiers dead. In return, 39 legionnaires lay dead in the hacienda. The terrible heat and wounds killed most of those remaining, including Maudet, despite Mexican attempts to save them. The few survivors who had run out of ammunition and mounted a bayonet charge were passed into captivity and later released. The relief column arrived at Camerone much too late to rescue any of Danjou's legionnaires. The men buried their dead comrades of 3rd Company, 2nd Battalion in a common grave. Danjou's wooden hand which had become separated from his body was picked up by a local rancher, who ➲

French Foreign Legion soldiers in their immaculate uniforms on Camerone Day (Dominique Pineiro/DPL)

For the Camerone parade each legionnaire's uniform must be immaculate, later they can celebrate. (FFL)

kept it as a souvenir for a couple of years before selling it back to General Achille Bazaine, the French commander in Mexico, himself a one-time Legion officer.

The Camerone Legacy

The battle at Camerone has become a Legion legend, symbolising everything that defines the modern-day force. April 30 remains the holy day of the Legion, Camerone Day. On this day, every year legionnaires are forgiven virtually any transgression short of murder, and the great deeds of the past are celebrated with much ceremony. On April 30, every year an officer or sergeant will select a junior legionnaire and that man will command his section for the day. This has seen sergeants and officers being assigned cleaning duties and being ordered to make legionnaires a coffee, but the limit of the junior soldier's power is always balanced by the fact that if he goes too far, he will pay the price the following day.

In 1931, General Paul Rollet, often described as the father of the Legion, instigated Camerone Day with a large formal ceremony at the Sidi-bel-Abbes barracks in Algeria. It included a march-past, led as usual by the Legion's bearded sappers, followed by speeches and a solemn parade of Danjou's hand. At the Monument aux Morts in Aubagne, the Legion still parades, and

A guard of honour escorts the Legion standard on Camerone Day. (FFL)

Bands will play throughout the day to mark this special event. (FFL)

A legionnaire with the Parachute Regiment on parade for Camerone Day in Corsica. (FFL)

a highly decorated former legionnaire has the honour of bearing Danjou's hand. The entire Legion stands to attention while an NCO reads the story of Camerone. The same ceremony is repeated wherever the Legion is stationed.

Camerone has become a verb as well as a noun. 'To Camerone' has come to mean making a last stand against enormous odds, with little hope of survival. One of the surviving Legion officers used the phrase at the bitter end of the French debacle at Dien Bien Phu in 1954, when the commanders in the valley considered whether to surrender or try to break out. He said: "You can do a Camerone with a hundred guys, but not with ten thousand." When the Legion left its spiritual home, Sidi-bel-Abbes, Algeria, in 1961, monuments were dismantled stone by stone and returned to France. At the same time, the Legion's treasured mementos were tenderly brought back to new places of honour in the regiment's museum. These items represent an immense military tradition, of absolute loyalty, unswerving courage, and contempt for death. ●

THE TRAINING BEGINS

The Legion – March or Die

The Legion's training barracks is located on the outskirts of Castelnaudary, a town in southern France, sometimes referred to by recruits as 'Castel'. Only recruits who have passed all the extra assessments, criminal checks, psychometric tests, and medicals at Aubagne will make their way to Toulouse railway station and onwards to the base. With new identities now confirmed, clothing and equipment issued, and contracts signed these volunteers are now members of the Legion. The train journey is around four and half hours, passing through Montpellier with glimpses of the Mediterranean coastline before the train heads inland to Toulouse. Here a coach will collect potential recruits and ferry them to the regiment's base, 30 miles southeast of the city.

The Legion wants people who are ready to devote themselves to the regiment in a five-year contract. Not all are running away from their past or alimony cases, a large proportion seek adventure, but this is not for thrill seekers.

The Legion's training barracks is located on the outskirts of Castelnaudary, a town in southern France. (FFL)

The railway station at Toulouse. This will be the last time the recruits experience civilisation for months. (Didier Descouens)

Instructors will use binoculars to locate recruits during camouflage and concealment exercises. (FFL)

Recruits live in clean but basic accommodation and will be expected to clean it every day. (Andy Darby/DPL)

The barracks at Castelnaudary is often busy with lorries taking recruits into the training programme. (Andy Darby/DPL)

Training is harsh, some say brutal and there is no forgiveness for failure. Castelnaudary is surrounded by countryside and at least four old 'farms' which are used by recruits during their four-month training course. The barracks at Castelnaudary, defines military excellence, the buildings are aligned like 'soldiers on parade' in exactly the right spot – even the trees are planted with symmetrical perfection. The base is also run with fanatical discipline by officers and soldiers of the 4th Foreign Infantry Regiment.

Quartier Captain Danjou

A large inscription at the main gate reminds all who enter of the importance of events in Mexico with the words Legion Estranger, Quartier Captain Danjou. A soldier dressed in full parade uniform and white Kepi oversees all arrivals and departures from a bulletproof observation post situated behind metal gates, which are closed at night. Every morning passers-by can see the changing of the guard as six legionnaires come off duty and another six commence their 24 hours on guard.

Rifles must be kept clean at all times, there is no excuse that the instructors will accept. (FFL)

Rookie legionnaires undergo constant training to make sure they can use the Legion's weapons. (FFL).

and adapted for use by the Legion, with living quarters, storage areas for equipment, as well as classrooms for indoor instruction. In several of these procured farms the large loft areas have been turned into accommodation with old bunk beds and damp mattresses or in some cases camp beds. Access to the recruits' loft is often via an external staircase, so as they do not pass the instructors' living areas. Corporals often rig a rope to an old barn hoist, which would have been used by farmers to lift straw bales up to the top floor. Recruits are given time to find a bed and then face their first task – climbing the rope to the loft, but they are not allowed to use their legs. Very few manage at the first attempt and after a week of struggling the instructors show the trainees the technique used to climb the rope. This challenge often becomes a daily routine in the morning and evening, to test the recruits and develop their physical capability.

The training area includes rolling countryside, woodlands, rivers, a deserted village for urban combat training, abandoned

The train journey is yet another opportunity, like the trip to Aubagne, for recruits to think about their future life in the Legion. Some will travel as a group and discuss stories they have heard about the training and the brutality. The mention of the word 'farm' generates fear among recruits. Stories of brutality and runs with heavy packs in the dead of night sometimes influence one or two to leave the train before it arrives in Toulouse. For those who are determined or who see very little future for themselves 'outside' due to a criminal past or personal circumstances, the Legion is now their family – providing they can pass the four months of training ahead of them and what some consider the 'unforgiving mentality' of instructors. If any abscond on the journey to Toulouse, having decided the Legion is not for them, they will be treated as deserters and if caught will face prison.

On arrival at the camp, recruits are marched to the parade ground. Here corporals will brief the new arrivals in French, from this point on all conversations in native languages are banned during the working day. It is at this point that non-French speakers are teamed up with someone who is fluent. There are always a number of French nationals, who officially cannot join, but list themselves as being from Monaco, Switzerland, or Canada as an excuse to get in. The first few days are based around the issue of additional equipment, extra fitness training and lectures about personal hygiene and other administrative matters. At meal times the recruits march to the dining hall as a formed group under the command of the duty corporal. The food is not hotel cuisine but is packed with calories. Chicken and rice with a baguette and black coffee is a favourite and recruits rarely leave any on the plate.

The Farm

Usually, two weeks after arriving at Castelnaudary the recruits will prepare their equipment and head for the 'farm'. The French Army has invested little money into these 'farm' camps which are spread across hundreds of acres and used as a base for recruits during their training. Once they were home to a flourishing agricultural businesses, but today they are a shadow of their former enterprise. Many of the main barns have been converted

The recruits are encouraged to look after each other and avoid calling on the medic all the time. (Andy Darby/DPL)

As training develops, the recruits will learn about close quarter fighting in buildings. (FFL).

tanks, and an obstacle course that covers several miles. Mental strength is vital here as the instructors will push recruits beyond their limits in an attempt to get rid of them. At each 'farm' there is a parade ground, often a small, cobbled area, while recruits learn the slow marching style that is unique to the Legion. It is more of a swagger compared to the stiff marching style of the British and American military. At the farm, the recruits also learn the Legion's marching songs that proclaim the glorious history of the Legion. Every night the recruits will sing and help improve their French, the most popular being *Le Boudin* – the official marching song of the regiment.

Tactical training involving section and company attacks are taught in phase one. (FFL)

Face, Feet and Fingers

Jim Muirhead, a Brit who joined the Legion in 2001, said the most important aspect of training is to look after your body. He said: "You need to think about face, feet, and fingers. Your teeth must be a priority and you need to avoid shaving rashes otherwise you will get a punishment for having a dirty razor. Your feet are critical to success, blisters, sores caused by tight fitting boots, and infections from ingrowing toenails can cause you incredible pain . Finally, fingers, there are loads of blokes who injured their hands and could not shoot well on the firing range, again this will get you a punishment. The Legion has a very singular approach to soldiering, their view is that you are here because you want to be, not because they want you – at least, not until you have passed training."

There is little sleep at the 'farm' and most recruits will lose 6-7 kilos during training. The instructors have what many might regard as 'unachievable expectations' – they will plan

The FAMAS French assault rifle was for many years the Legion's weapon of choice. (FFL).

Map reading is a key part of Legion training, recruits are not allowed to use GPS watches. (Yves Debay/DPL)

exercises in which recruits march all night, mount a dawn attack, and then complete an assault course before facing a French test in which each man must read aloud one part of the code of honour. Washing facilities are limited at the 'farm' but legionnaires will be expected to have clean clothes and shave every day – unless told otherwise. A normal day will on average include 250 press-ups, two sessions of physical training, followed by weapon training and tactical assessments. By the end of week four recruits will face15km runs. Earlier in the course trainees will face a 'loaded march' carrying their backpack and weapon and the distance will quickly increase. Instructors will show rookies how to present their equipment and clothing for inspection. Daily physical training and punishments will be introduced in an attempt to quickly weed out those they feel are not suited to the Legion. Rookies are up at dawn and as there is little transport, the trainees do what the Legion is good at and march everywhere. They will become

Marching with full equipment is a major part of Legion training. (FFL)

Physical training is a daily event and as training progresses it gets harder. (Andy Darby/DPL)

Advanced weapon training will involve learning about the Legion's anti-tank missile systems. (FFL)

As training nears the end, those who have performed well will be invited to join the REP in Corsica. (Yves Debay/DPL)

proficient in map reading, pass an assault course, learn about a number of different weapon systems and be ready to survive in the countryside.

Weapon of Choice

For many years, the FAMAS, a bullpup assault rifle, was the weapon of the regiment. It could fire up to 1,100 rounds a minute and was known by soldiers as the Bugle. The weapon uses a delayed blowback operating system that functions best with French-specified, steel-cased 5.56×45mm ammunition. Using standard 5.56mm NATO ammunition employed by other armies can create over-pressure and case ruptures in the FAMAS during extraction, which can lead to severe malfunctions. Consequently, the French military discreetly banned the use of foreign-produced ammunition in all French-issued FAMAS rifles.

Today the regiment has adopted the HK416F as the main assault rifle and the Glock Gen5 as a sidearm. The HK416F has a standard 30-round magazine, is known for its precision, reliability, and adaptability. The rifle has a maximum effective range of 300 to 500 metres, depending on the variant. It uses a short-stroke gas piston system, which reduces the carbon fouling in the chamber, improving reliability and reducing maintenance. The HK416F is also compatible with various accessories and modifications, making it a versatile choice for different combat scenarios. During tests, the HK416 fired 10,000 rounds in full-auto without malfunctioning. The Glock Gen5, a semi-automatic pistol with a magazine capacity of 17 rounds, and an effective range of around 50 metres, is the selected side arm used by the

Before the final week of tests, recruits will be reminded that they joined the Legion to serve France. (Yves Debay/DPL)

Others who deliver a strong performance will be invited to deploy to French Guiana. (FFL)

At the end of the kepi march, recruits enjoy a ceremony in the field before returning to barracks, . (Andy Darby/DPL)

Legion which recruits are trained on during the second phase of the course.

Rookies must carry their weapon with them everywhere while at the 'farm'. When asleep they learn to tie the rifle strap to their wrist to avoid instructors taking the weapon off them at night. If corporals manage to take a weapon the individual can expect a severe punishment. Training evolves as the course develops; recruits will be taught combat fighting, usually Thai or Jiujitsu. They will be told to hide in the countryside and then a sniper equipped with binoculars is tasked to locate them – those found too easily will face punishments.

The Legion loves to march and recruits will face at least four tests a week carrying heavy weights across distances which get longer and longer, starting with a short 'introduction' distance of three kilometres and quickly increasing in distance and pace to 45km. With all instruction in French, recruits quickly learn to understand the regular orders. As the pace of training ramps up, the company of recruits will be required to complete more press-ups and longer runs. The runs can range from an easy paced five kilometres to 20km runs at pace and often wearing boots. After two months of non-stop effort, the trainees will head back to 'Castel' to clean equipment and if they have performed well, they will get a four-hour pass to go into town.

Most will head straight to a restaurant and order a good meal after the limited quality of food at the farm. The weekend is in fact the half-way point of the four-month courses and instructors will ramp up the training. The marches are extended, more equipment is carried, and the pace quickens. At the end of the third month of recruit training the newcomers face a week of practical and written tests covering everything from shooting, weapons, explosives and mines, combat tactics, map reading, signals, first aid, maths, and French. This series of exams must be passed in order to give a recruit the right of passage to continue and undertake the final endurance test known as 'The Kepi March'.

The Kepi March

This is a four-day forced march which involves the trainees' tactics and procedures being tested as well. The route covers undulating

A recruit is congratulated by a Legion officer on the award of his white kepi. (Andy Darby/DPL).

Within months of completing training legionnaires can expect to be on operations. (Yves Debay/DPL)

terrain, roads, steep hills and is undertaken in all weathers. Many recruits suffer blisters and stress fractures, and the staff are looking for those men who will overcome the pain. In the US or UK military medics would insist that anyone suffering is withdrawn and given medical attention. The instructors encourage the mentality of no man will be left behind, unless seriously injured – in which case he will be taken back to the hospital in the barracks. Otherwise, he will be a quick given medical check, his equipment shared among his comrades and urged to carry on with the march. Blisters, stress fractures and exhaustion are regarded as routine. In one case a recruit's blisters were bleeding and his calves swollen to the extent that he was limping badly. The instructor halted the march and order the soldiers and his mates to sort his feet out and distribute his equipment. His feet strapped up he continued the last three miles.

On the final day of the march, the recruits will arrive at the finish – in some cases they hold a parade and are awarded their kepis in the field, in other circumstances they are driven back to Castelnaudary, and the ceremony takes place in the camp. The kepis are issued and fitted weeks before, each cap is then labelled with the legionnaire's names, sealed in a plastic bag, and stored away. In the final weeks before the 'kepi march' trainees must learn by heart to recite the Legion Code of Honour, which they will sing at the ceremony. At the end of the ceremony the colonel will give the order the order "Remise de la kepi". In one movement the trainees remove their green beret with the left hand, put it into the left trouser pocket and then place the kepi on with the right hand and salute – all movements done in silence. After the parade, the recruits will celebrate with a few beers and a lot of traditional singing.

A happy recruit in ceremonial dress after passing the four-month course. (Andy Darby/DPL)

In the following days, the newly qualified legionnaires will learn how well they did in training, those soldiers in the top third will be given the chance to choose which unit they go to – with the best often selecting to go to the REP, the Legion's Parachute Regiment. Others will be posted to the 2nd Foreign Infantry Regiment at Nîmes in France; the 3rd Foreign Infantry Regiment in French Guiana; the 13th Demi-Brigade in Djibouti; the 1st Foreign Cavalry Regiment at Orange (France) as well as the 1st and 2nd Foreign Engineer regiments based respectively at Laudun and Saint-Christol.

Newly qualified legionnaires wearing their white kepis. (FFL)

Since formation the Legion's soldiers have deployed across the globe to fight for and defend the French Republic. (Yves Debay/DPL)

THE EXPENDABLES

The formation of the French Foreign Legion

The French Foreign Legion has a unique approach to combat which has shaped the regiment's ethos. They prefer death to dishonour and in battle these soldiers accept that they are expendable in the name of the Legion. From famous battles to its passionate music and marching songs, the Legion has a 'cult status' in which recruits accept the indoctrination into this regiment of strangers, or they quickly leave. It remains devoid of 21st century 'social etiquette' and openly states that it trains to kill the enemies of France. Legionnaires live by a code of honour, that states kill or be killed, and demands the absolute loyalty of each Legionnaire to the regiment. They have, since their creation, been an organisation which adapts and overcomes in the most austere conditions. On operations they represent France, but they fight for each other, their reputation, and the coveted white kepi.

At the Legion's base in Aubagne, the wooden hand of Capt Danjou is a reminder of the Legion's ethos. Next to the regimental artefacts in the ceremonial room is a bronze bust of King Louis-Philippe – a lasting tribute to the monarch who created the regiment in March 1831. He wanted to bolster the country's military at a time of an expanding French empire and decided to accept regular soldiers from all across Europe who were left unemployed after the French Revolutionary Wars and had sought refuge in France. To expedite the recruitment of foreigners who had fled their country with no papers, the French government authorised that any volunteers could be hired into the Legion with

A bust of King Louis-Philippe at Aubagne – a lasting tribute to the monarch who created the regiment in March 1831. (Portrait by Louise Adélaïde Desnos, 1838)

The Legion's approach to combat has shaped its ethos into a sacred order of fighting men. (Yves Debay/DPL)

Just months after formation the Legion sailed for Algeria in August 1831, tasked to boost the garrison in North Africa. (FFL)

a simple declaration of their identity. A law was established on March 9, 1831, which contained two essential principles that still exist. These are that a volunteer will serve in an overseas role and there is the option to enlist under a pseudonym, otherwise known as a 'declared identity'.

First Deployments

Just months after formation, in August 1831 the Legion sailed for Algeria, tasked to boost the garrison in North Africa, which regular French troops had seized a year earlier on July 5, 1830. The initial years of the regiment saw thousands of Legionnaires based in Algeria where regular French officers had little enthusiasm to command in what was seen as an unpopular posting. The Foreign Legion initially struggled with a lack of experienced non-commissioned officers, corporals, and sergeants, to command legionnaires. The Legion was organised into a single regiment of seven battalions. Each one followed the same format of a regular French Army line infantry battalion: structured on eight companies of 112 men each and formed of men from specific nationalities or linguistic groups. For example: the 1st Battalion was composed of veterans of the Swiss Guards and the former French Hohenlohe Regiment, the 2nd and 3rd Battalions were composed of Swiss and German volunteers, the 4th Battalion consisted of soldiers of Spanish extraction, the 5th Battalion were mostly a mixture of Sardinians and Italians, the 6th Battalion was formed of Belgians and Dutch, and the 7th Battalion formed from volunteers of Polish origin.

With the Spanish Civil War looming in 1834, Spain asked the French government to disband the 4th Battalion of the Legion, so that they might return to their homeland in the service of their country. The 7th Battalion, composed of Polish volunteers, was thereafter re-designated as the 4th Battalion.

By early 1854 the regiment was rebuilding its manpower and in June of that year received orders to send five battalions to serve in the Crimea campaign. The previous year, France had joined forces with Great Britain in the Crimean War, defending the Ottoman Empire against Russia, and now needed more troops. The French ship *Jean Bart* ferried four battalions to the Crimean Peninsula, a fifth was held at Gallipoli as a brigade reserve. In total eight companies drawn from both regiments of the Foreign Legion took part in the Battle of Alma in September 1854. It was a significant victory for the French and British force.

The Bonifacio monument commemorating the soldiers of the Legion killed on duty for France in the North African campaign and at the battle of El-Moungar in North Africa. (Jean-Pol Grandmont)

By early 1854 the regiment was rebuilding its manpower and in June of that year received orders to send five battalions to serve in the Crimea campaign where they fought at the battle of Malakoff. (FFL Museum - William Simpson)

More legionnaires arrived to bring the contingent up to brigade strength and as the 'Foreign Brigade' it served in the Siege of Sevastopol during the winter of 1854 and 1855. It was here that the Russians nicknamed the Legion the 'leather-bellies' after the large cartridge belts that soldiers wore attached to their waists. The siege was the culminating struggle for the strategic Russian port and was the final episode in the Crimean War. However, the Legion lacked equipment, suffered terribly in the cold winter months of the siege, and was hit by cholera which killed more than 200 of their number.

In the early 1860s the Legion found themselves in Mexico after the south American administration suspended all payments to the country's foreign creditors. The deployment resulted in the now legendary last stand by Captain Danjou and his legionnaires at Camerone. Then, during the Franco-Prussian War of 1870 between the Second French Empire and the North German Confederation, the Legion were called onto the streets of France. According to French law the Legion was not to be used within Metropolitan France and thus, it was not a part of Napoleon III's Imperial Army that capitulated at Sedan.

On October 11, 1870, two provisional battalions disembarked via sea at Toulon, it was the first time the Foreign Legion had been deployed in France itself. It attempted to lift the Siege of Paris by breaking through the German lines and succeeded in retaking Orléans but failed to break the siege. Then on March 18, 1871, when the regular army tried to remove cannons from an artillery park on Montmartre, National Guard units resisted and killed two army generals. On the same day the Legion assisted in suppressing the Paris Commune uprising.

French soldiers of the Legion pictured in the Tonkin region of northern Vietnam. (FFL)

Eight companies of legionnaires took part in the Battle of Alma in September 1854. (FFL Museum)

Son Tay where some of the fiercest fighting took place during the Indochina War. (FFL)

Legionnaires walk towards a French Transall C-160 aircraft on a French military base in Djibouti. (US Army)

The American poet Alan Seeger who served with the Legion. (FFL)

In 1883 the troops from the Foreign Legion sailed to Tonkin, the northern region of Vietnam, and took part in hostilities that preceded the Sino-French war in August 1884 and ended in April 1885. The Legion's soldiers then formed part of the attack column that stormed the western gate of Són Tau on December 16. Throughout the conflict the Legion continued to fight and in January 1885 the Foreign Legion's 4th Battalion was deployed to the French bridgehead at Keelung (Jilong) in Formosa (Taiwan), where it took part in the later battles of the Keelung campaign.

Africa

The French Foreign Legion had played a major role in the expansion of French power across Africa and the growth of the country's colonial empire in the Sub Saharan region. From Algeria to the west coast both French culture and influence dominated. People spoke the language, learnt about the country's history in schools, and many men fought in the French African Army.

By 1890 France was moving towards the establishment of a French protectorate over Morocco which caused resentment across the ➲

An artist's impression of the uniform of the Foreign Legion's 4th Battalion when deployed to the French bridgehead at Keelung where it took part in the later battles of the Vietnam campaign. (FFL)

Review of the Marching Regiment of the Foreign Legion (RMLE) at the end of November 1918. (FFL)

The Viet Minh on parade in Hanoi 1945. (Vietnam government)

Legionnaire's assault a German position in North Africa at the battle of Bir Hakeim in 1942. (FFL)

Cao Bang today, during the Indo China conflict the Viet Minh inflicted heavy losses on the Legion here. (Yves Debay/DPL)

A legionnaire with a Vet Minh prisoner. (FFL)

indigenous population. Italy, Spain, and Britain also had interests in Morocco and feared France was seeking total control. Consequently, each country sought to police its own area of the country. Tribesmen, often travelling in groups of more than 900, fought back attacking Legion outposts and French dignitaries.

By the beginning of the 20th century, French troops in the region faced numerous incidents, attacks and looting by armed groups of Moroccan tribesmen in the west of Algeria.

Since their first arrival in north Africa, the Legion had contributed to the expansion of the French colonial empire supporting the control of trade in nearby Morocco. By 1890 France was moving towards the establishment of of a French protectorate over the country which caused resentment across the indigenous population. Italy, Spain, and Britain had interest in Morocco and feared France was seeking total control. Consequently, each country sought to police its own area of influence. Tribesmen, often travelling in groups of more than 900, fought back attacking Legion outposts and French dignitaries. In August 1903 more than 1,000 tribesmen attacked a contingent of the French Foreign Legion at the town of Taghit just inside Algeria in the battle of El-Moungar of what became known as the South Oranese campaign. For three days, the legionnaire force, which consisted of 148 soldiers from the 22nd Mounted Company of the 2nd Foreign Legion Infantry Regiment, repelled repeated attacks of an enemy more than 10 times their number, and inflicted heavy losses on the attackers.

The officers and most of the non-commissioned officers were killed in the first stage of the fight. Quartermaster-Sergeant Paul Tisserand, who commanded the survivors, sent two cavalrymen attached to the Legion to Taghit for reinforcements. About 40 survivors of the French force gathered on a nearby hill and under a scorching sun and without water, fought off the enemy for more than eight hours. Near the end of the battle, Tisserand, who was seriously wounded, gave over command to Corporal Detz - the highest-ranked man still able to fight. Late in the afternoon they were relieved by Captain de Sulbielle, who rode

On November 20, 1953, the Legion launched Operation Castor in which four battalions of paras were dropped into Dien Bien Phu. (FFL)

from Taghit with his cavalry. At the sight of the approaching French troops, the Moroccans retreated in small groups. Total French losses amounted to 38 dead and 46 wounded. A presidential decree granted to all survivors of the battle the Colonial Medal, and Tisserand was promoted to lieutenant.

The World Wars

The Legion was unaware that within a few years it would be fighting across Europe in the bloody trenches of World War One. Among their number was American Fred Zinn, an aviator of German descent from Battle Creek in Michigan. He was a qualified aviator and while visiting France in 1914 he joined the Legion serving on the Western Front until February 1916 where he was wounded for a second time in an artillery attack. Zinn later transferred to the French aviation unit.

After the declaration of war in August 1914, a call was made by the administration in Paris for foreigners residing in France to support their adopted country. While many would have preferred direct enlistment in the regular French Army, the law prevented foreigners from joining the regular army leaving only the option of serving with the Foreign Legion.

Just days after conflict was announced a reported 8,000 volunteers applied to enlist in the Legion's Paris recruiting office in a single day.

The Foreign Legion fought in many critical battles on the Western Front during what became known as the 'Great War' and although it played a smaller role in

The French used USAF aircraft with French insignia on to drop paratroopers over Dien Ben Phu. (FFL)

mainland Europe during World War Two, it was active in North Africa. The 13th Demi Brigade formed for service in Norway, found itself in the UK at the time of the French Armistice and in June 1940 it was deployed with the British 8th Army in North Africa and distinguished itself in the Battle of Bir Hakeim in 1942.

Prior to World War Two, France had governed Laos, Vietnam, and Cambodia in what was known as Indochina. Following the fall of France on June 25, 1940, these areas fell under the administration of the Vichy government and their Axis partners, including Imperial Japan who already had their eyes on the region. In March 1945, Japanese forces in the Lang Son area of northern Vietnam demanded the formal surrender of French troops including legionnaires and when their commander, General Emile Lemonnier refused, he was beheaded. A camp in the former French colony of Djibouti now bears his name – Camp Lemonnier.

The Viet Minh had emerged in strength from World War Two and by the end of the war France was losing control of its colony. But Paris was ready to fight for it and in late 1945, with the defeat of the Japanese Empire, the first French troops were back in Indochina, now partially occupied by the Viet Minh. A formal agreement between the French government and the movement ended in December 1946, when the Viet Minh launched an attack at French garrisons. China and Russia supported the Viet Minh, while the French enjoyed support from the United States. The Legion was now attracting new recruits - many French speaking former German soldiers joined the Foreign Legion to pursue a military career after the war, an option no longer possible in Germany. This included French German soldiers from the Alsace-Lorraine region who had been forced conscripted. These former German soldiers made up as much as 60% of the Legion during the war in Indochina. Contrary to popular belief however, French policy was to exclude former members of the Waffen SS.

Vietnam

By late 1950, Viet Minh roadblocks, mines, and ambushes along Route 4 had inflicted heavy losses on French troops and equipment heading for the French base at Cao Bang.

This route was vital to French Colonial Forces and the Viet Minh poured ten battalions into the area to ensure they controlled the route, also known as Highway 4, to isolate the French and cut-off their supply columns.

The French began supplying the region by air and opted to evacuate all but four bases. Then the French attacked the town of Thai Nguyen on Colonial Route 3. The raid was actually a deception to allow the garrison at Cao Bang to be evacuated south along Route 4 on foot but thousands of Viet Minh attacked as the 3rd Foreign Legion Infantry Regiment started its withdrawal - their route was blocked by the Viet Minh. At Dong Khe 300 defenders of the 5th and 6th companies, 2nd Battalion, 3rd Foreign Legion Infantry Regiment faced overwhelming odds and the garrison was decimated as 140 legionnaires were captured with the rest dead or missing.

The Viet Minh now achieved victory after victory against the French as China supplied them with more and more weapons and the Viet Minh maintained their control of supply routes. By 1951 the French were facing significant fighting, and the Legion was huge taking causalities. General Jean Marie De Lattre de Tassigny established a defensive line around Hanoi effectively closing off the area against the Gulf of Tonkin. Called the 'De Lattre line' this series of fortifications slowed down the Viet Minh, at least for a short time.

By 1953 the French had intelligence that the enemy were planning to seize Dien Bien Phu and deployed 13 battalions to the area in response. On the night of November 20, the French launched Operation Castor in which four battalions of paratroopers, including those from the Legion were dropped into the area. In addition, the 13th Dem-Brigade comprising the 3rd and 5th Legion regiments were sent in as part of the ground force. However, the Viet Minh were aware of

A French Foreign Legion mortar crew at Dien Bien Phu. (FFL)

Legion paratroopers pictured in Indochina hauling a wheeled mortar. (FFL)

the operation and had a plan to trap and destroy the French. At night, more than 60,000 Viet Minh engineers-built roads to allow heavy weapons to be moved forward, they hauled artillery guns and ammunition into camouflaged positions and amassed ammunition dumps – all under shelter of the natural tree line and out of sight of the French. Long range weapons were hauled onto high features and set to fire at predetermined targets - again hidden from sight. Finally, an army of labourers built the first line of trenches and tunnels that would be used against the offensive.

On March 13, 1954, the battle of Dien Bien Phu began and as shellfire rained down on the French positions the monsoon season started bringing torrential storms. The French faced terrible losses and in April the brigade reserve from the 2nd Battalion of Estranger Parachutists jumped in to join their comrades. With them were 750 legionnaires from the 3rd and 5th Regiments - who had never parachuted – it was the only way in as the airfield was closed. The fight waged on until May 7 when the Viet Minh had overrun most of the French positions apart from a base named Isabelle. The Legion commander at a forward command post ordered the artillery guns at Isabelle to open fire on his own position rather than surrender.

Dien Bien Phu had been a lesson in tactics and strategy and was the decisive battle of the war. The battle had cost the Legion more than 7,000 dead and wounded. In France, radio stations across the country played solemn music as the nation paid tribute to those who died.

During the Indochina War, the Legion suffered the loss of 10,283 of its own men in combat. The 1st Battalion Estranger Battalion(1er BEP) particularly distinguished itself, while almost being annihilated twice. It was renamed the 1st Foreign Parachute Regiment

French legionnaires in the trenches at Dien Bien Phu. (FFL)

Captured French soldiers from Dien Bien Phu, escorted by Vietnamese troops, are marched to a prisoner-of-war camp. (Vietnam government)

(1er REP). For the French army, Dien Bien Phu is a painful reminder of its failure. This terrible French defeat brought the country to a standstill. Politicians questioned the military's strategy and international allies feared French foreign policy would be more cautious and withdraw from intervention operations. In France, opposition to the war in Indochina caused turmoil that foreshadowed the upheavals and divisions in America following the introduction of US forces in Vietnam a decade later. By the end of the eight-year war, more than 77,000 French-led troops were listed as killed or missing in action, with more than 84,000 wounded. Of those troops killed or missing, about 60% were Vietnamese, Cambodians or Laotians fighting on the French side, and most of the rest were non-Frenchmen in the Foreign Legion or African battalions drawn from French colonies. Only about 15% were French nationals.

According to French historians, the Viet Minh took nearly 40,000 prisoners from 1946 to 1954, of which almost 30,000 were never returned. Many Vietnamese fighting on the French side were killed by their captors, the French say. After the fall of Dien Bien Phu, the French pulled out of the region. Concerned about regional instability, the United States became increasingly committed to countering communist nationalists in Indochina. The United States would not pull out of Vietnam for another 20 years. ●

The French deployed a small number of US-supplied M24 Chaffee light tanks during the Indochina campaign. (FFL)

OUT OF ALGERIA

The end of Algeria and post-colonial conflicts

Algeria is regarded as the spiritual home of the French Foreign Legion. For many decades Paris deployed legionnaires here where they trained and stood at readiness to defend the country's colonial empire. The north African country had been under French control since the 1830s and after World War Two France sought to maintain its cultural grip and sovereignty. But a growing number of Algerians wanted independence – an issue France was not prepared to consider. In May 1945 demonstrations took place across the country demanding self- rule. Violence erupted against French Algerians and the government in Paris sent the French Army to reinforce the Legion and quell the protests.

By 1954 the French had been defeated in Indochina while Tunisia and Morocco were also pressing for autonomy. The Legion had returned to its homeland in Algeria to lick its wounds and recover from its losses in southeast Asia. But instead, the force faced a growing conflict on its doorstep. Thousands of Algerians who had fought for the French felt that their commitment and loyalty should now be rewarded, and their country allowed to govern itself. France refused to compromise and stated that Algeria would remain French. Inspired by the defeat of French forces in Vietnam, Algerian revolutionaries formed the Front de Libération Nationale (FNL) and launched a campaign to remove the colonial rulers.

In November 1954, the FNL mounted its first attack killing six Europeans in the remote Allures mountains. The FNL called themselves outlaws (fellagha) and were soon dubbed the 'Fell' by the Legion. In December 1955, they attacked the eastern city of Constantine where many French citizens lived, killing 49 civilians. They set fire to schools, farms, and houses - in fact, anything that represented France. The government in Paris was outraged and wanted to send a message that this violence would not be tolerated. In a swift revenge campaign French forces killed more than 2,000 suspected fellagha before the end of the year.

The fighting was brutal and the attacks indiscriminate with the FNL killing French civilians and settlers as well as the military. The men of the 1st REP, the Legion's parachute battalion, was at the forefront of the conflict. These men, like all legionnaires, believed that

The harsh Algerian Saharan desert was the training ground for the Legion in Algeria. (Algeria TB)

For many decades Paris deployed legionnaires to Algeria where they trained and stood at readiness to defend the country's colonial empire. (FFL)

Algeria was sacred land, it had Legion blood in it and should never be abandoned. The regimental cemetery in Algeria was full of the fallen from operations in Indochina, Morocco, and Tunisia.

Following his return to power in 1958, General de Gaulle had single-mindedly pursued the same foreign policy he had adopted during his previous administration. He saw France as a proud, sovereign, and independent great power participating as an equal among the leading world nations. His instinct was to retain control of Algeria, but his administration could not manoeuvre a political outcome that retained sovereignty while appeasing the Algerian nationalists. France saw Algeria as a key part of its empire and many even considered it part of France. Giving it up meant losing valuable resources and prestige. Algeria was closely tied to French culture through settlers, called Pied-Noirs, who had lived there for generations. But de Gaulle quickly saw the Algerian problem could not be resolved with political influence or military strategy and feared a conflict would consume resources. His resolve was to cut

Legionnaires at the battle of Habra in Algeria in 1835. (Horace Vernet)

The rugged Algerian mountain range provided ideal training opportunities for the Legion. (Algerian TB)

away, but to make sure France was seen as fair, and not running away from north Africa, he announced a vote on independence.

The President's view that Algerians had the right to democratic self-rule was not welcomed by the French military in Algeria or the settlers. There was a growing feeling among the Legion that the plan in Paris to give up Algeria was a sell-out and an insult to the honour of the Legion. A growing number of people now wanted to stop de Gaulle's plan.

Far Right

In the January 1961 referendum the majority of French people voted in favour of Algerian independence. Citizens living abroad and in the military were allowed to vote although French settlers abstained in quiet protest. Following the vote, a far-right group emerged, calling itself the Organisation Armée Secrète (OAS) . This secret army was formed by a small number of French politicians and military officers with the aim of retaining colonial rule in Algeria and blocking de Gaulle's initiative to approve independence. The military officers who included Generals Maurice Challe, André Zeller, and Raoul Salan were opposed to Algerian self-rule and believed that the country should remain a colony. They claimed President de Gaulle was giving away French sovereignty and accused the government in Paris of treason and abandoning French Algerian colonists and loyal Muslims.

A legionnaire in blue serge coat and kepi in Algeria in 1852. (Ernest Meyer)

The aim of the 1836 Battle of Constantine was to conquer the Algerian city, but the attack was a French failure. (FFL)

Legionnaires in combat during fighting in Morocco. (FFL)

A legionnaire wearing desert uniform in late 1882. (FFL)

The OAS was seen as a far-right French dissident group and branded a terrorist organisation. It carried out bombings and assassinations in an attempt to prevent the implementation of de Gaulle's plan and the group included former legionnaires. General Yves Godard, a paratrooper and former leader of the French resistance in World War Two France, was chief of operations. His single most famous success was to smash a 100-strong French Army commando unit sent to Algeria by de Gaulle to end the OAS attacks.

At the heart of the military operation was the Commando Delta, the enforcement wing of the OAS. It was run by Legion deserter Lieutenant Roger Degueldre, and his devoted aide Bobby Dovecar. Degueldre used an assumed name, stating his nationality was Belgian, but no one really knew. In Indochina he had established a reputation for being at the forefront of operations against the Viet Minh. He gained rapid promotion to sergeant and after saving a colonel's life, he rose further to adjutant chief and volunteered for the paras. Degueldre became one of the most decorated sergeants in the Legion and received direct promotion to lieutenant in the field, an act that is very rare.

Never far away from Degueldre in Algeria was Bobby Dovecar, a young man with

Legionnaires in the Moroccan desert in 1921. (FFL Museum)

only three years Legion service. He was of Yugoslavian birth and an exceptionally good legionnaire. He had reached the rank of sergeant within a couple of years – no mean feat as any legionnaire will attest.

Official French records show that in January 1962, 364 people were killed and 624 wounded in an OAS killing spree, aimed at wrecking the peace plan. Their wider aim was to generate a full-scale uprising of Algerian Arabs seeking independence against the French settlers and in turn force the French government to protect the Europeans and force Paris to abandon plans to leave the country. On January 23, ten OAS bombs exploded in Paris, one of which wounded and disfigured a four-year-old child, causing outrage in the city. President de Gaulle announced new measures, banning all newspapers from reporting about the OAS as well as increasing the presence of armed troops on the streets of Paris to more than 25,000. In late February, de Gaulle ordered 40,000 more troops to be sent to Algiers to crush the OAS terrorists after they killed a dozen Algerians in one day. In addition, a secret French government intelligence force known as C-Group stepped up its activities in Algeria. They had been sent by de Gaulle's government to break the OAS. They operated from their own remote barracks, employed several Algerians who could amass local intelligence, and by the end of February the force had rounded up more than 600 OAS men and bagged 642 automatic firearms, 10,000 rounds of ammunition and a cache of documents.

The Generals' Coup

Throughout March there was concern among the senior ranks of the Legion and the regular army about de Gaulle. On April 22, 1961, a group of French generals in Algeria mounted a coup . They were not part of the OAS, but they sought change. During the night,

A French legionnaire machine gun team in Morocco where the colonial power faced demands for independence. (FFL)

French legionnaires paraded in Algiers in post-war years. (FFL)

The Algerian nationalist army which sought independence from France. (FFL)

President Charles de Gaulle had wanted to retain Algeria, but opted for a public referendum, (FFL)

The badge of the OAS. (FFL)

the 1st Foreign Parachute Regiment, which comprised 1,000 men, took control of all of strategic points across Algiers in just three hours. They were supported by other Legion units, but the action was mainly taken by men serving with 1st REP. A separate plan was made for the Legion's additional parachute regiments to capture strategic targets in France, but this element of the operation never took place. As anger soared, a small group of legionnaires had decided they would assassinate President de Gaulle when it was announced he was to visit the Legion. The plans were foiled when French secret service agents changed the route of the visit and the men concerned were arrested. A large number of number soldiers in the 1st REP were detained along with their officers – some of whom were later executed.

In Paris, de Gaulle ordered a state of emergency fearing other legionnaires may join the coup. Both airports in Paris were sealed off by the military, armoured vehicles were deployed at the Elysée Palace, and a naval blockade of Algeria was imposed. A furious de Gaulle called for the Legion to be dismissed and the French media slammed the regiment supporting calls for it to be axed. There was sympathy from other Legion units - these men in the 1st REP had fought hard in Vietnam, their regiment had twice been close to being wiped out, and their call to save Algeria for France was respected. But their actions had put the future of the regiment at risk. It was a dark day for the regiment, and many feared for the future of the Legion. As President de Gaulle pressed for tough action defence chiefs negotiated with ministers and compromise was reached. The 1st REP was to be disbanded and the Legion reduced in strength from 200,000 men to 10,000. Additionally, all of the remaining regiments were to be dispersed throughout the French dominions to French Guyana in South America, Tahiti, Djibouti, Mayotte, and Corsica and it was agreed that the headquarters would eventually move from Algiers to Aubagne near Marseille in southern France.

The demise of the 1st REP sent a wave of concern across the Legion. Recruitment was halted for several years and President de Gaulle, never a fan of the supporter of the regiment, maintained his distance. The coup remained an embarrassment to the Legion's high command, but in Algeria the OAS attacks continued across the major cities as talks proceeded to conclude independence for Algeria. At the beginning of March 1962, the provisional Algerian government formally signed what became known as the Evian Peace Agreement under which France effectively relinquished its authority over the country and promised a phased departure of its military forces.

On March 26, in response to the shooting of seven French army conscripts by the OAS the French army launched a ruthless offensive. Their first success was to capture the former general, Edmond Jouhaud, one of the four OAS supreme commanders. He was seized after a seven-hour battle between infantry and tanks of the French army on the militants' stronghold. Then more than 100 French settlers, who had no part in the fighting, were killed and another 200 wounded when French troops opened fire on what was supposed to be a peaceful demonstration.

Another OAS team, consisting of nine ex-Legion officers and 86 soldiers, retreated into the mountains where they came under attack from FLN fighters.

Roger Degueldre, a former legionnaire who joined the OAS. (FFL)

Maurice Challe was a French general during the Algerian war and one of four generals who took part in the coup. (FFL)

Capture and Castigation

In the first three weeks of April, the three most wanted OAS men were captured. First, Dovecar was caught in a villa owned by a wealthy Algerian, then Degueldre was detained and tried to convince the authorities they had the wrong person. He calmly presented false identity papers but was immediately recognised at police headquarters. The third was Raoul Salan; the man who had brought his country to the brink of civil war. He was arrested in a first-floor apartment in Algiers. In a surprise move he escaped the death sentence at his military tribunal in Paris. He was represented by the ultra-right barrister Maitre Tixier-Vignancour who had also defended Marshal Pétain after the war – the French officer who had collaborated with German forces. Many believed that Salan was not sentenced to death after the OAS issued a statement warning they would kill the judges if he was executed. Former legionnaire Bobby Dovecar had no such escape. During his career he had been honoured three times for bravery in action, but his unblemished record was little help in court. He was sentenced to death by

From left to right: French generals André Zeller, Edmond Jouhaud, Raoul Salan, and Maurice Challe during the coup. (FFL)

The planned departure from Algeria was brought forward after negotiations broke down and the Legion left within days of Christmas 1970, many packing into Transvaal aircraft (FFL)

firing squad. As his executioners took aim, he defiantly shouted at them: "Vive la Légion."

On June 8, the defiant OAS blew up Algerian oilfields deep in the Sahara and then they firebombed Algiers University in a vain scorched-earth attempt to halt the handover of Algeria. A month later on July 3, French rule was formally ended after a referendum in Algeria, at which 99% of the population voted in favour of an independent Algeria after 132 years of French control. The exodus of Europeans began immediately, but even as they prepared to leave, they came attack fire from the FLN. Hundreds were massacred in revenge attacks by Arab gunmen.

By the time the former legionnaire Roger Degueldre faced his trial, the battle for Algeria was all but over, and he was to be de Gaulle's symbolic offering to the peace process. He remained silent throughout the hearing, simply sat with his piercing eyes fixed on the tribunal head, General de Larminat. However, the Legion, still looked after its own. The death sentence on 36-year-old Degueldre was carried out on the morning of July 6,1962 – a date many veterans remember. The firing squad of legionnaires stood as Degueldre was marched out before them. An NCO marched the firing squad to their positions, but he was a regular army sergeant, who had taken the place of the squad commander normally filled by a Legion officer. Degueldre looked at the firing squad and shouted: "Do your duty." In a defiant distraction he then began to sing *The Marseillaise*. The volley of shots rang out, echoing around the courtyard and Degueldre slumped forward but

Edmond Jules René Jouhaud was one of four French generals who briefly staged a coup in Algeria in April 1961. (FFL)

he was not dead. Only one of the eight bullets had hit him, in the shoulder. A serious wound but certainly not fatal. Questions were later asked as to how seven fine Legion marksmen could miss and only one hit the condemned man and still not kill him. It was left to the NCO, Sergeant Prideaux, to deliver the 'mercy shot' from his own pistol. There was obvious suspicion that the Legion marksmen had deliberately missed, and each was questioned but no action taken. Degueldre was dead.

The Aftermath

When the peace agreements were signed, France sacked more than 150,000 African soldiers who had served with the Armée d'Afrique – France's African Army. The retribution in North Africa that resulted from France's treatment of the anti-communist Algerian soldiers was seen by many as a final despicable chapter in the whole affair. France not only left the country it had plundered but betrayed those among the indigenous population who had supported French rule to the last, and who were now killed for doing so.

The new Algerian government had agreed that France could withdraw its forces gradually with the last Legion units due to leave in 1972. Then on Christmas Eve 1970, an Air Force general arrived in Algeria. An order quickly followed for all officers to assemble in the cinema. The general made an announcement which stunned those listening. He informed them that negotiations between France and Algeria about the future presence of French bases in Algeria had broken down. He told them that the base was to be evacuated immediately, adding that an air bridge had been established and that flights would commence the following day – Christmas Day. Paris ordered that the evacuation must be completed by 1800 hours, December 28 and directed that the Legion would provide security and be the last to leave.

Many French Air Force, and civilian staff who had been there for some time had pressing questions about personal possessions. Many of them had motor cars and personal items such as furniture, clothes, and children's toys. But the order was

Sergeant Bobby Dovecar was another legionnaire who had joined the OAS. (FFL)

When it was clear that they were leaving Algeria, the Legion dismantled their monuments and send them back to France. Others in the air force and regular army left it too late when the sudden departure came at Christmas 1970. (FFL)

clear, everyone was to leave by 1800 hours on December 28, and what could not be carried in a suitcase could not be taken. All military equipment was to be removed and items that were too large destroyed.

The legionnaires had one last fling, a brief and unusually drink-free Christmas meal then they started to evacuate. The departure was fraught and fast. As the last legionnaires boarded the final aircraft an officer hauled down the French and the Legion flags, declining to pay any respect to the waiting Algerians dignitaries who stood watching. He marched aboard the aircraft and saluted Algeria. As he did so a senior sergeant threw a bottle of Kronenberg onto the runway – the favourite tipple of the regiment and a Legion farewell to the country they had called home. The legion officer was later summoned before French Army chiefs to explain why he had not saluted the Algerian officers.

It is estimated by the Algerian government and the FLN that nearly eight years of revolution had left more than 700,000 dead. Some other French and Algerian sources later put the figure as high as 960,000. French military authorities listed their losses at nearly

In response to the generals coup, both airports in Paris were sealed off by the military and armoured vehicles were deployed at the Elysée Palace (FFL)

Many French Foreign Legion vehicles were abandoned as the order was made to leave Algeria within a few days. (FFL)

The French North African medal awarded for operation service in Algeria. (FFL)

25,000 dead and 65,000 wounded. For many senior legionnaires Algeria remains the spiritual home of the Legion and de Gaulle's decision in 1959 that the Algerians had the right to determine their own future has never been accepted or forgiven. The veterans still claim that under French Colonial rule Algeria was a peaceful thriving country.

OUT OF AREA

The Legion has long been used as the global protector of French interests

A Legion officer's safety equipment is checked by a Mexican marine prior to an amphibious exercise. The two forces were adversaries back in the 1800s and they now collaborate in regular exercises. (SHANE JACKSON/US Navy)

OPERATIONS

The Legion also deployed to French Polynesia in the late 1960s to help build the necessary infrastructure for the French nuclear tests. (French Govt)

Since its formation the French Foreign Legion has been deployed on out of area operations, protecting the country's interests and when required fighting for France. The departure from North Africa forced changes and new deployments for the Legion to overseas territories, in Madagascar and then in Guiana, Djibouti, French Polynesia and the archipelago of the Comoros Islands.

The 5th Foreign Regiment was created in French Polynesia to help build the necessary infrastructure for the French nuclear tests carried out in the late 1960s. In Guyana, the 3rd Foreign Infantry Regiment helped build the launch site at the Guiana Space Centre. The impact of de Gaulle's decision to disband the 1st REP after the failed coup still stung and many hardened legionnaires questioned if ➲

The Legion has established a jungle warfare school deep in the rain forest of French Guiana. (FFL)

The nuclear tests in French Polynesia were conducted in conjunction with the United States and the UK. (US Govt)

Among many global postings the Legion has deployed to Djibouti where it established a base. (Yves Debay/DPL)

The departure from North Africa forced changes and new deployments for the Legion, including French Guiana. (FFL)

Paris would continue to use the Legion as a 'high readiness force' or slowly dismantle it. But the public held the Legion in high esteem, and politicians knew that any move to retire the country's most prestigious force would not be welcomed by voters and send the wrong message across the globe to those countries who quietly respected the reputation of the Legion as the 'strong arm' of France's military power.

Within a few years of leaving Algeria the Legion was back in action. Chad, a former French colony, had won independence from France in 1960. Then in 1965 civil war erupted, and an insurgent group called the Frolinat emerged with the intent of overthrowing President Francois Tombalbaye. By 1968 the revolt had spread across the country and the insurgent force had grown to more than 3,000. Chad had agreed a Defence Accord with France in 1964 in which in extreme circumstances French troops would be sent to help the African government. Tombalbaye sought help and President Charles de Gaulle who was still in office approved the intervention of a French force, spearheaded by the Legion.

In French Guiana, the Legion protect the European Space Centre, from where the Ariane 5 rocket made more than 80 successful launches. (European Space Agency)

Legionnaires fit American parachutes at Kinshasa airport prior to their 1978 assault on Kolwezi in Zaire. (FFL)

The mission, codenamed Operation Bison, quickly restored security and by July 1971 the intervention ended.

Peacekeeping

Then, in 1978 the Legion found itself in a new role of peacekeeping, something the Legion was not familiar with. The 2e REP was sent to Lebanon to support a civil and military mission set up by the United Nations to restore peace and stability in the Middle Eastern country. Known as the United Nations Interim Force in Lebanon (UNIFIL), it was set up to counter the destabilisation of Lebanon by armed groups belonging to the Palestine Liberation Organisation (PLO), which were carrying out actions against Israel in the late 1970s. It was a deployment the Legion neither liked nor enjoyed.

In the same year trouble flared in Africa when the Front for the National Liberation of the Congo (FLNC) invaded Zaire. The offensive on May 13, involved more than 4,000 Katangese rebels who attacked the town of Kolwezi, an important mining centre in the Katanga Province in southern Zaire. The militants, calling themselves the Tigers, aligned themselves with the left wing Congolese FLNC in neighbouring Angola which was led by Nathanael Mbumba. The political aim of the FLNC was to occupy the Katanga Province, a region particularly rich in cobalt and copper, and separate it from Zaire. The then President of Zaire, General Joseph Mobutu, sought help from Belgium, France, Morocco, and the United States in a bid to restore order in Kolwezi and stop the violence spreading across the country. In the early in the hours of May 16, 1978, the Legion's 2nd Foreign Parachute Regiment was put on alert for operations. The French feared any delay would risk details of the plan being leaked ➲

The regiment has sent soldiers to multiple locations across Africa and to hotspots in the Middle East. (Yves Debay/DPL)

The REP flew to Kolwezi for Operation Bonite aboard four C-130s and a Transall C-160 aircraft. (FFL)

As Operation Bonite was put together at very short notice, the legionnaires needed to borrow American T-10 canopies and use them for the first time. (FFL)

to the press and compromise the operation so, on the following day, May 17, soldiers of the 2e REP were flown from Corsica to Kinshasa and preparations commenced for what was to be a parachute assault.

Battle for Kolwezi

Because of the hurried departure the Legion needed to borrow parachutes and at Kinshasa military airport the 2e REP was instructed in the use of American T-10 parachutes. Planning continued and on May 19 the 2e REP took off from Kinshasa at 11am bound for the town of Kolwezi, 930 miles away. They mounted the mission, codenamed Operation Bonite, in five military aircraft: four Lockheed C-130 Hercules of the Zairian Army and a Transall C-160 of the French Air Force. At 3:15pm, the legionnaires jumped onto the objective, an open flat area almost 800 metres long and which commanders had listed as Drop Zone Alpha. It was near the centre of Kolwezi and situated between a hotel and the police station. Each Hercules had 80 legionnaires on board, and they dropped from port and starboard doors in a process known as 'sim-sticks' using the US Army parachutes for the first time. On

C-130s of the Zairian military supported the Legion's operation into Kolwezi by the 2e REP. (FFL)

Paratroopers exiting a C-160 Transall, using US T-10 canopies. (FFL)

the ground, they quickly assembled in their units – although six legionnaires had already been injured by small arms fire from rebels on the ground. Corporal Robert Arnold, a young British member of the 1st Company was missing. The next day, he was found to have been killed by rebels, still equipped with his parachute. Corporal Arnold became the first legionnaire killed during Operation Bonite.

REP mortar crew in Kolwezi just hours after the regiment had jumped in with all their equipment. (FFL)

Following the drop into Zaire, Corporal Robert Arnold, a young British member of the 1st Company was missing. He had been killed by rebels and when found his parachute was still with his body. (Yves Debay/DPL)

Once inside the town, the 2e REP quickly secured several strategic points; the 1st Company moved into the Jean XXIII Lycée (a high school), the 2nd Company held the hospital and Gecamines Factory, while the 3rd Company moved towards the Impala Hotel which the rebels were using as their headquarters. The rebels were holding hostages at the Lycée school and hospital and a fleet of vehicles at the Gecamines Factory were seized and allowed the legionnaires to become mobile. In addition to their initial task the 3rd Company was ordered to carry out another two missions. First, they had to seize a train station in the centre of Kolwezi, and then, an important bridge located between the Old Town and the New Town.

Fighting began the minute the REP entered the town and continued in all the main streets for several hours. At 3pm, rebel armour attempted a counterattack with three captured Panhard AML armoured cars, which the legionnaires eliminated with rocket and small arms fire. The lead AML was knocked out at a range of 50 metres by an LRASC F1 anti-tank missile. By 5:45pm all strategic points were seized, and the town of Kolwezi was under the control of the 2e REP. A day later on May 20, at 6.30am another wave of 250 paratroopers was dropped east of the city, cutting off rebel positions from behind and by noon this part of the area was also under Legion control. This area was known as the P2 quarter and as the REP entered, they discovered the massacres that had occurred there. The day after the airport was retaken, President Mobutu arrived in person to boost troop morale and reassure the population; he seized the opportunity to parade several European corpses. This struck Western public opinion and led to a widespread acceptance of the decision by the French government to launch the operation. Later it was alleged that the Europeans had in fact been executed by troops of Colonel Bosange because Mobutu wished to provoke an international intervention.

In a follow-up action the town of Metalkat, later renamed Metal-Shaba, was taken by the 2 REP, forcing 200 rebels to withdraw. Sergeant-Chef Daniel was killed during the fight but within two days, the entire city and surrounding area was under control. The REP rescued 2,800 Europeans and evacuated them on May 21.

The Panhard used by rebels to ambush the legionnaires during Operation Bonite. (FFL)

After the initial jump into Kolwezi for Operation Bonite the REP secured the town, mounting roadblocks around the area. (FFL)

After the departure from Algeria, the 3rd Regiment moved to French Guiana where they have been based since 1973. (FFL)

The battle for Kolwezi demonstrated the ability of the Legion to deploy parachute trained troops at short notice and carry out rescue missions and is often used on British and American military command courses as an example of fast and successful intervention. The FLNC lost more than 400 killed and 160 taken prisoners while at least 100 people were massacred. The 2 REP lost five killed and 25 wounded. It is estimated that 700 African civilians and 170 Europeans were killed during the entire operation.

Beirut

In 1982 the Legion was back in the Lebanon as the 2 REP deployed to Beirut as part of a multi-national force to protect French nationals during the Lebanese civil war. In the same year the Legion recorded its biggest loss of life since the Battle of Dien Bien Phu when 36 paratroopers and French marines died in an accident in Djibouti. The soldiers serving with the 2eREP were taking part in routine exercises in Djibouti with a group of French Marines when their plane was lost in bad weather and crashed in the foothills of the Mont Garbi, a mountain range in the western region of the Tadourag area of the country. All 36 men on board died in the accident. Earlier in 1976 Djibouti had been the scene of another accident in which six legionnaires died when their Puma helicopter crashed on an exercise.

The 3rd Foreign Infantry Regiment, the 3e Régiment étranger d'infanterie is the most decorated regiment of the Foreign Legion and as such when re-organisation of the Legion took pace following the departure from Algeria it was sent to French Guiana. The regiment was created in 1915 from the veterans of the 2nd, 3rd, and 4th Marching Regiments of the 1st Foreign Regiment and distinguished itself during World War One at the siege of de Belloy-en-Santerre in the Somme. On July 4, 1916, around 2,000 legionnaires attacked fortified German positions in the occupied village. It was a brutal fight in which the Legion lost more than two hundred soldiers. Among the dead was Alan Seeger, the American poet who had joined the Legion. After the war, a square in the village was renamed in his memory.

On September 14, 1918, the regiment took part in the Battle of Vauxaillon in

For the Kolwezi operation heavy lorries were 'borrowed' locally, and a number of Legion vehicles flown in by C-130. (FFL)

Legionnaires take part in what is regarded as the toughest jungle warfare course in the world. (Yves Debay/DPL)

northeastern France on the Western Front. This was significant as the French were able to break Germany's Hindenburg Line, a German defensive position built in the winter of 1916-1917. However, at least 275 men of the regiment were killed during the battle and a further 1,158 men were wounded. After the war the regiment was based in Morocco from 1920 and in World War Two fought the Germans across North Africa with major operations taking place in the Mansour mountains in Tunisia. Later, in 1944 the regiment joined forces with the French Army's 5th Armoured Division and saw action across the Rhine and into Austria.

At the end of the war the regiment received numerous citations and the Croix de Guerre – the French cross for valour. It also received the US Distinguished Unit Citation with the inscription 'Rhine Bavarian-Alps'. After the war the unit was renamed the 3rd Foreign Infantry Regiment and moved back to Morocco, before moving to Indochina in late 1945. And, in 1948 a parachute company of the regiment was established to support operations and joined the 1st Parachute Chasseur Regiment of the French Army in a force known as the 3rd Indochina Air Infantry battalion. Stationed at Hanoi the parachute company took part in airborne operations including Dông Khê and Diên Biên Phu.

Following a series of courageous combat action operations, the company was dissolved on May 31, 1949. In the Indochina campaign, the regiment, which had been enhanced for the deployment, lost more than 2,000 men. In December 1954, the regiment sailed back to Bone in Algeria and in 1962 was sent to Madagascar where it became expert in jungle warfare.

The jungle threats include tarantulas, electric eels, and jaguars. (Carlos Valenzuela)

Operation Titan

Then, on September 11, 1973, the 3rd Foreign Infantry Regiment was re-deployed for a permanent role in French Guiana. Here the Amazon rainforest covers 95% of the country's area and comprises more than 1,200 species of trees, including numerous precious woods. France occupied the territory in the 17th Century along with Dutch and Spanish settlers. Until the 1930s, France sent convicts to penal colonies in French Guiana, including the notorious Devil's Island. Today another former penal settlement, Kourou, is home to a European Space Agency rocket launch site. It is this sensitive and secret site that the Legion is assigned to protect in a mission known as Operation Titan.

The protection of the space centre involves deep patrols into the jungle to ensure no 'adversaries' can get close to the base. Operating in the forests is hard work. The canopy of trees, vines and bushes shield the ground from direct daylight and generate a constant humidity. The jungle of French Guiana is home to some of the world's most dangerous animals – including the pit viper and coral snake. Rivers can contain electric eels and piranhas while the area is also home to tarantulas, poison dart frogs and many other deadly species which make daily life a challenge.

The jungle warfare course includes crossing rivers – which are packed with dangers. (Yves Debay/DPL)

Attack dogs, mainly Malinois, are trained and used in French Guiana to boost the security capability. (FFL)

Jungle Warfare

It is here that the Legion has established the military's most respected jungle warfare centre. Every year it holds two eight-week long events at the jungle warfare centre called the Jaguar Course which are attended by legionnaires from other regiments as well as US and British soldiers, one of which was a Grenadier Guards unit in 2021.

New arrivals to the 3rd Regiment in Guiana face a short period of 'jungle theory' training and will then deploy into the humid terrain to learn how to build a shelter, catch food, and survive in the damp environment of swamps and dense vegetation. They need to learn to avoid the dangers that can kill them such caimans, spiders, and jaguars. This 'baptism of fire' leaves many legionnaires, who deploy here for two years, either loving or hating the jungle. The Legion operates on the border between French Guiana and Brazil, regarded as one of nature's most hostile environments for man to live and fight.

For many Legionnaires French Guiana is the hardest posting of any of the regiment overseas deployments. The French colony sits on the northeast coast of South America between Brazil and Suriname. The legion operates on the border between French Guiana and Brazil in the jungle which sits between the Maroni and Oyapock rivers. The limited roads can quickly vanish under the growth of vegetation and rivers can swell in heavy rains, changing the shape of the landscape. French Guiana also has substantial resources including gold, iron, bauxite, and diamonds which in recent years has attracted illegal gold prospectors from Columbia and Brazil seeking their fortune. These gold miners often use vast quantities of chemicals as they wash stones which pollutes the rivers.

The mission to counter this illegal activity is codenamed Operation Harpie and involves the regiment operating in support of the Gendarmerie to combat the gold prospectors

The deadly coral snake is among many reptiles found in the jungle. (Carlos Valenzuela)

as well as to bring calm to the country. The intervention came after Jean-Bertrand Aristide resigned as Haitian President and fled into exile following a coup. The legionnaires also deployed to Cap-Haitien, Haiti's second-largest city where a street gang that had begun the armed rebellion that helped oust President Aristide refused to disarm. In a 2010 referendum, voters rejected the option of increased autonomy but today, like many South American countries in the north of the continent, French Guiana is facing an influx of illegal immigrants from Brazil and Suriname.

After Hurricane Irma hit the Caribbean island of Saint Martin in September 2015, legionnaires from the 3rd French Infantry Regiment based in French Guiana, were sent to support rescue operations. A total of 150 legionnaires from 2nd Company, arrived in Martinique to help French nationals and islanders on the world's smallest inhabited island divided between two nations - France and the Netherlands.

Today, the Legion's 3rd Foreign Infantry Regiment is France's on-call rapid reaction force in South America, while protecting the European Space Centre, countering illegal gold mining, and maintaining a jungle warfare school which has developed a reputation as a world leader. ●

who operate in large armed groups to mine parts of the jungle. Patrols of 30 legionnaires deploy on 20-day missions to find the miners and carry bergens with equipment to survive and live in the jungle which includes everything from the chainsaw to the explosives. In the dense virgin jungle, they often take a day to progress less than 500 metres. If anything goes wrong the team must look after themselves, it is impossible to send a helicopter as the jungle vegetation is too thick. A third area of the Legion's role is to patrol the Oyapock river to identify illegal tree clearing and mining teams.

In the 1990s, street violence erupted in French Guiana, partly fuelled by high youth unemployment, and political tensions with Paris after local people alleged a lack of investment in the country's economy by France. A total of 23 people were arrested and while the Legion were put on standby to reinforce the local Gendarmerie, they weren't required. Then on June 27, 2003, Nahel Merzouk, a 17-year-old unarmed French citizen of Algerian and Moroccan descent, was fatally shot by police after being stopped for a traffic violation in Nanterre, an area in the west of Paris.

The police initially justified the shooting, citing safety concerns, but conflicting accounts emerged on social media sparking riots. The unrest on the mainland sparked further violence in French overseas territories, particularly in French Guiana. One government worker was killed by a stray bullet and police officers faced gunfire. Again, as in 1990 the subject of economic investment and socio-economic challenges, as well as alleged oppression by the government were raised as factors which added to the public disorder. Thankfully, on this occasion the Legion was not called on to become involved.

In 2004, elements of the 3rd Foreign Infantry Regiment were deployed from French Guina to Haiti in Operation Carbet. More than 150 soldiers arrived in the main Haitian city of Port-au-Prince to secure French diplomatic interests and national citizens

The jungle base in French Guiana is also used to train some of the Legion's specialist divers who move ashore and find a route ahead of the main body of troops. (Yves Debay/DPL)

DIVERSE DEPLOYMENTS

The Gulf War and the new world order

The start of the 1990s saw conflict in the Gulf and the collapse of the Soviet Union. Both events generated a flood of recruits to the Legion but the fall of the Berlin Wall in particular meant that many of these would-be legionnaires came a from eastern Europe, which changed the composition of the regiment for the next decade. The end of the Cold War had acted as a catalyst for conflict in regions where Moscow had been politically dominant and inspired opposition groups to call for change. But this was not just across eastern Europe. In Africa former French colonies from Algeria to Morocco, Chad, and Gabon now faced uprising as the Legion faced a new world order of operations.

In 1989 Russian had withdrawn from Afghanistan and during Iraq's war with Iran, Moscow had supported Baghdad, and supplied arms to Saddam Hussein. Iraq had borrowed the revenue from several Gulf States to pay for its war and had amassed huge debts. When the war ended, the dictator called on the United Arab Emirates and Kuwait to cancel the debts owed by his administration. The Iraqi leader argued that the loans should be considered payments to Iraq for protecting the Arabian Peninsula from Iranian expansionism, but his appeals went unanswered. By early 1990 Iraq's economy was close to collapse and Saddam Hussein needed to generate revenue. A plan to seize Kuwait had allegedly been drawn up during the summer of 1990 and then on August 2, at about 2am local time, Iraqi forces stormed Kuwait. By annexing Kuwait, Iraq gained control of 20% of the world's oil reserves and, for the first time, a substantial coastline on the Persian Gulf.

The same day, as the United Nations Security Council unanimously denounced the action, Western leaders created a Coalition force, spearheaded by Arab nations, to eject Iraqi forces. France put its military at readiness and by September the French mission headed by the Legion, and codenamed Operation Daguet, was heading for the desert. Legionnaires sailed from Toulon aboard a requisitioned cruise ship along with French Army paratroopers and armoured units. By late October 1990 they were in the Saudi desert preparing to take part in ➲

AMX-10RC vehicles of the Legion's Cavalry units were a key weapon in the advance through Kuwait as part of Desert Storm. (DPL)

Armoured VAB personnel carriers arrive in the Middle East in preparation for potential operations. (Andy Darby/DPL)

In addition to their AMX-RC10s, Legion Cavalry squadrons are equipped with the Panhard wheeled armoured car. (DPL)

AMX-30 main battle tanks of the regular French Army supported the Legion during Operation Desert Storm. (DPL)

Iraqi forces quickly collapsed under the onslaught of Desert Storm and as they retreated, they set fire to the oil wells. (DPL)

manoeuvres with Coalition forces in readiness for the potential advance into Kuwait.

The Legion force comprised the 1st Foreign Regiment, the 1st Foreign Cavalry Regiment, elements of the 2nd Foreign Parachute Regiment, the 2nd Foreign Infantry Regiment, and The Legion's engineers. They were all attached to the 6th Light Armoured Division whose mission was to protect the Coalition's left flank. While the the 6th Foreign Engineer Regiment operated in support of the 82nd Airborne. The Legion's tank regiment arrived by sea and was immediately deployed on the Saudi-Iraq border and operated as one unit.

Soldiers lived in the desert and quickly established a routine of train, eat, sleep, repeat. As Christmas approached legionnaires built a church – the legion is largely Catholic – and on Christmas day held a special service. As part of regimental tradition every soldier is given a present and the most junior legionnaires are invited to sit at the top table and eat Christmas dinner with their commanders.

As word came that Saddam refused to withdraw his forces, the ground operation was now ready. The church was dismantled in deference to their Saudi hosts, and the focus

The Desert Storm advance starts as legionnaires wearing chemical clothing prepare for action. (Andy Darby/DPL)

French and US troops inspect a bombed Iraqi T-69 during Desert Storm. (DPL)

now directed towards nuclear, biological, and chemical (NBC) warfare training after fears that Saddam's forces would deploy weapons of mass destruction. Legionnaires ate and worked in chemical warfare clothing and respirators to ensure they could respond and survive a chemical attack.

US General Norman Schwarzkopf praised the role of the Legion in the Gulf war. (DPL)

Desert Storm

Air strikes were mounted throughout early February as the Coalition waited for ground hostilities to start. Finally on February 23, 1991, the Legion's regiments moved off from their start line heading north and west of Kuwait, along with 4th Company of the 2nd Legion Infantry Regiment (2eme REl).

They travelled in armoured vehicles and wore chemical warfare clothing with their colleagues from the 1st Legion Cavalry Regiment (1er REC) heading the advance. The task given to the Division Daguet, which was composed of units drawn from more than 25 French Army regiments, was the capture of the Al Salman air base some 150km inside Iraqi territory in the west.

The Legion's VAB armoured personnel carriers also act as mobile command platforms. (DPL)

As they advanced, the legionnaires secured two intermediate objectives, designated as 'Rochambeau' and 'Chambord'. Iraqi forces were overwhelmed, and the mission accomplished in less than 48 hours - crushing Saddam's elite 45th Mechanized infantry Division. The Al-Salman airfield was taken on the afternoon of February 25 and the nearby village on the morning of February 26 without resistance. The advance to the airport took place at pace and was protected by armour from the French Army who deployed AMX-30 tanks, AMX-10RCs and ERC-90 Sagaie with most

Destroyed Iraqi armour littered the battlefields of Desert Storm. (DPL)

of the legionnaires traveling in VAB armoured personnel carriers.

The Iraqi command and logistics were paralysed as their communications were destroyed during the legionnaires' aggressive advance. Iraqi troops surrendered in their thousands without putting up a fight with the volume of prisoners forcing the Legion to build holding areas. Under the pressure of international opinion, the offensive finally halted without Coalition forces advancing on Baghdad and the wider force halted just north of Kuwait. Defeated, Saddam Hussein's forces withdrew from Kuwait, sabotaging oil wells as they went. By the end of the operation, France had suffered no battle casualties, except for two men who were killed in an accident. The ground offensive ended on February 28, after Iraq accepted all UN resolutions. The Legion had moved fast and after the conflict General Norman Schwarzkopf, commander-in-chief of allied forces during Desert Storm praised their actions, saying: "Few people know that at the end of the first day of the ground attack, after having made a fantastic breakthrough, the French forces were the furthest north, the furthest west. They were the ones who had penetrated the deepest into Iraq. They successfully accomplished the missions that were assigned to them and did so in a tremendous way."

Gabon

Prior to the Iraqi operation, in May 1990 the 2nd Company 2e REP had been sent to the former French Colony of Gabon, a country

The smoke from the oilfields caused problems for Coalition aircraft who could not see the enemy. (DPL)

Kuwaiti families celebrate the end of the conflict known as the First Gulf War. (DPL)

on the Atlantic coast of Central Africa. Across Africa, former French colonies were now facing rebellions as opposition groups sought new political administrations and their form of a new world order. The deployment of the REP followed political turmoil and violent demonstrations as well as widespread strikes across the country. Economic discontent in April had provoked demonstrations by students and workers. In response to grievances by workers, Omar Bongo, the country's leader, negotiated with them on a sector-by-sector basis, making wage concessions. Paris feared that French citizens could be trapped in the violence and the 2e REP evacuated more than 2,000 French nationals in a mission codenamed Operation Requin.

Then, in October, as a large number of Legion units sat in the Saudi Arabian desert waiting for the Coalition advance to commence, violence erupted in Rwanda. The rebel group, the Rwandan Patriotic Front (RPF), composed of Tutsi refugees, invaded northern Rwanda from their base in nearby Uganda. The RPF condemned the Hutu-dominated government for failing to resolve the problems faced by the refugees. France immediately responded by sending the 2e REP from the Central African Republic to Rwanda, to evacuate about 700 European nationals in a mission codenamed Operation Noroit.

A major threat during the Balkan wars was from military groups armed with surface to air missiles. (Yves Debay/DPL)

A Legion armoured patrol in Sarajevo during deployment as part of the United Nations Protection Force (UNPROFOR). (DPL)

The centre of the city of Sarajevo was destroyed during the early 1990s . (DPL)

Buses, buildings, and entire streets were destroyed in the main street dubbed sniper alley. (NATO)

French Foreign Legion soldiers acting as United Nations peacekeepers stand next to Red Cross-liveried armoured personnel carriers (APCs) in the midst of war damaged Sarajevo. (Sgt Michael Haggerty, US DoD)

EUROPE

Europe was now impacted by the actions in Moscow and the Legion were set for a new role. The collapse of communism in Eastern Europe, the unification of Germany a year later, and the demise of Soviet influence had all served to erode Yugoslavia's political stability. On April 5, 1992, the government of Bosnia declared its independence from Yugoslavia. The creation of an independent Bosnian nation that would have a Bosniak majority was opposed by Bosnian Serbs, who launched a military campaign to secure territory and 'cleanse' Bosnia of its Muslims. The subsequent civil war lasted from 1992 to 1995 and NATO forces were deployed as part of a United Nations peacekeeping force with the Legion heading an operation in Sarajevo – which had seen some of the worst violence. Elements of the 2e REP arrived in Sarajevo the capital of Bosnia and Herzegovina in October 1992.

At the same time, another company of the REP was sent to Somalia in support of a United Nations operation to facilitate humanitarian relief operations into Mogadishu, which was codenamed Operation Oryx. It worked alongside the US 'Restore Hope' mission.

Immediately following Desert Storm, the Legion found itself in the Balkans with the REP being deployed to Sarajevo. (DPL)

Sarajevo siege life. Local people collect firewood and precious loaves of bread. (Christian Maréchal)

UNPROFOR

By January 1993, the regiment had established itself in Sarajevo as part of the United Nations Protection Force (UNPROFOR). The REP's role was to protect the Sarajevo airport and provide security for the distribution of humanitarian aid within the city and its adjacent sectors, as well as to escort military and civil authorities. It was the first time that the REP had been forced to exchange their berets for blue peacekeeping helmets . A few weeks after their arrival, on February 11, the paratroopers suffered their first fatality. After having transported a woman in labour to a nearby hospital, Legionnaire Benko was killed by a mortar attack. He was the first combat loss for the 2e REP since the operation at Kolwezi in 1978. A second soldier, Legionnaire Nowakowski lost his leg. This incident prompted the government to propose the 'Français par le sang versé' (French by blood spilt) law, which from 1999 ensured that French citizenship would automatically be granted to any legionnaire seriously wounded during an operation, regardless of the length of their service.

The 2e REP also forced the international authorities to allow them to use return fire when under attack. (The UN forces were prohibited from using weapons.) The Balkans deployment was not a popular operation with legionnaires, who found themselves constantly turning back Bosnians, Serbs, Muslims, and Croats who tried to cross Sarajevo airport.

In June 1994, the Legion had returned to Rwanda on a humanitarian task, following the brutal genocide that occurred between April and June during the Rwandan Civil War. The French military launched Operation Turquoise which saw the deployment of legionnaires from the 2e REI, 13e DBLE, and 6e REG and the 2e REP's commando unit. Their task was to establish and secure a peace zone where tens of thousands of Tutsi refugees could find safety and security. In November 1995, the entire 2e REP (less the 1st Company) returned to Bosnia and Herzegovina in the former Yugoslavia for a NATO-led multinational peace enforcement mission, which was titled the Implementation Force (IFOR), known as Operation Joint Endeavour within the Alliance and as Operation Salamandre by the Legion. Stationed mainly between Mostar and Mont Igman (venue of the 1984 Winter Olympics), the REP was reinforced with 1er REC men, they maintained the task of ensuring the implementation of peace accords signed between Bosniaks, Serbs, and Croats. More than 1,000 para-legionnaires no longer wore the blue beret or helmet and were allowed to use their firearms.

In May 1996, the Legion was heading back to the Central African Republic after yet another African coup. The crisis stemmed from widespread public discontent over social and economic problems exacerbated by prolonged non-payment of salary arrears. The violence left 50 dead and almost 280 wounded. France reacted by sending the 2e REI and 1er REC to restore calm and prepare to evacuate French nationals in a mission called Operation Almandin. A peace accord was signed between the administration and opposition forces, then in November, a more serious third mutiny broke out, with the mutineers demanding the President's resignation.

Again, French soldiers, this time including the REP Commandos were deployed to ensure the safety of French nationals and foreigners in the country as part of Operation Almandin 2. On January 4, 1997, two French marines (a captain and a warrant officer) were killed by a rebel soldier with a burst from a submachine gun while they were negotiating in Bangui, the capital. In a follow-up operation, the REP's 4th Company and attached French marines attacked and captured the rebel barracks, killing nine rebel soldiers and capturing more than 20. The Legion briefly reinforced its forces before withdrawing to Corsica.

Republic of Congo

In May 1997, the Legion was back in Africa, deployed to the Republic of Congo (Congo-Brazzaville). It was tasked with evacuating French and foreign nationals as well as Rwandan refugees from neighbouring Zaire (where the 1978 Kolwezi battle had taken place). The mission was named Operation

The Congolese capital Brazzaville from where the Legion evacuated French Nationals in 1997. (Prevel Epotta)

A Legion VAB armoured personnel carrier with the United Nations Protection Force (UNPROFOR) passes the Presidency building in Sarajevo. (Christian Maréchal)

Serb families forced from their homes due to regulations in the Dayton agreement from 1995 - legionnaires found this work very frustrating. (Benjamin Andrea)

Pelican and was supported for a brief time by American, British, Belgian, and Portuguese forces. Calm was initially restored before violence erupted in Brazzaville between militias representing three presidential candidates. For three days, in early June 1997 heavily armed fighters fought and killed each other and devastated the infrastructure across the Congolese capital, killing hundreds of civilians. The Legion launched an operation to evacuate French nationals and on June 7, as the first evacuation mission was underway, a group of legionnaires escorting evacuees was fired on by rebels armed with heavy machine guns. A sergeant and a legionnaire were seriously wounded and as Legion Corporal Gobin tried to rescue his comrades, he was killed. The skirmish lasted an hour before the enemy was eliminated. The fighting was intense and had left an officer, a sergeant and two legionnaires wounded. Nevertheless, the operation was successfully completed and more than 6,000 foreign citizens, including an estimated 1,500 French nationals, were evacuated through the Brazzaville Airport by June 15.

Back in the Balkans

In July 1999, the 2e REP deployed for the third and last time to Bosnia and Herzegovina, now as part of the Stabilisation Force (SFOR), a NATO-led multinational peacekeeping mission. They returned to their Calvi headquarters in November. Then, after the attacks on the United States in 2001, the Legion was sent onto the streets of France as part of the government's Operation Vigipirate response plan to protect the country from Islamic attacks.

When Emmanuelle Macron was elected, he made it clear that French interventions in Africa, such as Operation Barkhane in Mali, were over. (French Armed Forces)

As the Legion underwent a further re-organisation the dissolution of the 5th Foreign Regiment in French Polynesia had been confirmed in early 2000. Between April and June 2000, the elements of the REP were sent to Kosovo in the former Yugoslavia following the 1998-1999 Kosovo War between Serbia and its separatist region. The deployment was part of the NATO-led peacekeeping Kosovo Force (KFOR), also known in France as Operation Trident. The company's task was to monitor and guard the only bridge in the town of Mitrovica to prevent the Kosovo Albanian and Serbian ethnic groups from attacking each other. This police-like mission to pacify angry crowds without using violence was another new experience for legionnaires. Here they had to stand and take abuse and often face violence from both communities while not responding – it was challenge for a regiment that is bred to fight.

Changing Times

In the late 1990s the Legion benefitted from more investment in equipment, including light infantry weapons and support weapons such as anti-tank systems. On July 1, 1999, the 2nd Foreign Engineer Regiment was created at the air base near Saint Christol, north of Marseille, – a

The Legion often found itself escorting UN humanitarian aid convoys. (Pals Paal Sarensen)

move that perhaps President de Gaulle would not have approved of. The regiment would become a mechanised combat engineer unit, assigned to the 27th Mountain Infantry Brigade (27e BIM) in support of infantry units on operations, and specialised in mountain warfare. At the end of the 20th century the Legion was preparing for the next change – a war against Islamic terrorism which would target France at home and abroad. But future French intervention in Africa was to be suddenly stopped when Emmanuelle Macron became President. His predecessors, including François Hollande, Nicolas Sarkozy, Jacques Chirac, and François Mitterrand, had all launched new French military operations on the African continent, often to safeguard French nationals or reinforce the security forces of former colonies. When Emmanuelle Macron was elected, he made it clear that interventions in Africa were over. He was the first French President born after the colonial era and made it clear that France had turned the page of postcolonial interventionism. When he took office, the Legion was deployed in Mali. His predecessor, François Hollande, had approved the operation to target Islamist extremists in Mali, Chad, and Niger, with a mandate to operate across borders. Macron ended it. The Legion continues to mount training in Africa and is ready to support national emergencies, but the new President was increasingly of the view that France's former colonies must resolve their own issues.

Elements of the French Foreign Legion remain in Africa on training teams and based in Djibouti but French intervention in former colonial countries is over according to the current French administration. (French Armed Forces)

THE REP

The Legion's Paratroopers

The Legion's premier unit is the 2nd Foreign Parachute Regiment, often referred to simply as the REP it is the regiment's only airborne unit and delivers the special operations capability to move anywhere at short notice. Within military circles it is held in high esteem and no more so than for its for its bold parachute assault into Kolwezi which undoubtedly saved lives even though its soldiers jumped into Zaire using parachutes they had only trained with for a few hours.

Raised in 1955, it is the successor to the 2nd Foreign Parachute Battalion, which fought in French Indochina and served alongside the 1st Foreign Parachute Regiment – which was disbanded by President de Gaulle's government after a military coup in Algeria. After France agreed to Algerian independence the REP base moved to Corsica in 1967 and from here it has been regularly sent on operations in Bosnia, Rwanda, Chad, Zaire, the Ivory Coast, Iraq, and Afghanistan as well as more recently in the Sahel. The relatively high pay and the prestige of being in an elite unit makes the regiment a popular choice for Legionnaires when they pass out of training at Castelnaudary. However, only the best recruits are accepted for service with the REP. ➲

French Legion soldiers from the REP jumping with the UK Parachute Regiment. (Dilip Banerjee/DPL)

Legionnaires from the REP jumping with US and German troops during a NATO exercise. (US DoD)

The REP has soldiers trained in mountain and arctic warfare who maintain their skills in the French Alps. (Yves Debay/DPL)

The REP's capability includes an amphibious company trained in all aspects of maritime operations. (Yves Debay/DPL)

Small inflatables can be used to ferry a company group of men at speed. (Yves Debay/DPL)

The C-130 Hercules remains the workhouse of the REP's parachuting capability, along with the C-160 Transall. (Yves Debay/DPL)

The Legion's amphibious force includes a specialist diving unit. (Yves Debay/DPL)

French Foreign Legionnaires armed with HK416 F rifles on the Bastille Day Parade in 2022. (French Armed Forces)

Historically the regiment has always had a large number of British and German volunteers, often men who have served in the British Army and have the adrenaline bug for more combat. Selection for unit takes four weeks at Camp Raffalli in Corsica with the first two weeks focused on physical tests followed by a further two weeks parachute training and then six jumps. The Legion's para training is known as 'promotion' or 'the promo' and while the entire course is listed at four-weeks, it can be longer depending on the weather and aircraft availability.

The REP serves within the French Army's 11th Parachute Brigade – but the Legion is the only force which trains its own paratroopers, the Army's 11th Para send their soldiers to the French airborne school at Pau.

A specialist diver marks a safe route ashore, clearing it of any IEDS. (Yves Debay/DPL)

The Legion train with the French Navy, deploying light vehicles which can drive up onto a beachhead. (Yves Debay/DPL)

Those serving in the amphibious unit must undergo sea survival training. (Yves Debay/DPL)

Those legionnaires selected at Castelnaudary for the REP are collected by an NCO from Calvi and escorted to the REP base. They travel by ferry to Corsica and are taken by bus to the barracks, usually on a Saturday morning. During the first week of 'promotion' the future legionnaire paratroopers still have to pass a series of tests unique to the REP – if they fail, they risk being returned to Castelnuadary. There are many traditions in the regiment and Camp Raffalli is no exception. There are three roll calls a day. The first, early in the morning, the second after lunch, and the last at 9pm. Another tradition is that a legionnaire is confined to the island for the first year of his first posting there. A third requires the entire regiment to march across the island from one side to the other once a year - a distance of about 200 kilometres.

The initial contract with the REP is for two years, but many legionnaires choose to stay longer. The regiment is frequently away on operational deployments, normally for four months at a time. Career promotion is slow, and courses are harder since the competition is tougher in such a small unit. Within the unit is the Commando force, formally known as the 'Groupe de Commandos Parachutists'. It is a reconnaissance troop, which parachutes ahead of the main legion battalion to identify a suitable drop zone for the main force. It trains in a wide spectrum of explosives and counter terror skills which include hostage rescue from buildings and aircraft. But only non-commissioned officers can apply to serve in the Commando unit. Members of the REP wear the winged dagger cap badge and a red Fourragere (Lanyard). The regiment is divided into eight companies and consists of 1,300 officers and legionnaires. Some non-Legion NCOs and females from the French Army serve with the unit in administrative roles, but they do not wear any Legion insignía. The REP's eight company groups each have a specialist skill. The specialities include urban, mountain, amphibious. or desert warfare as well as explosives and demolition. And there is an anti-tank missile force armed with the Akeron

A French jump master serving with the REP prepares to parachute from a French C-130 Transall aircraft near Camp Lemonier, Djibouti. (US DoD)

The ability to ski and move quickly across snowfields is paramount for those in the mountain and cold weather warfare unit. (Yves Debay/DPL)

MP (formerly MMP) system. Two further companies deliver sniper capability and a highly trained Commando team.

The mountain cadre often trains in the French Alps mounting long range ski-patrols, learning to survive in snow and ice. Legionnaires can volunteer for the High Mountain Team Leader Course which often takes place alongside the 2nd Foreign Engineer Regiment. Desert warfare again requires soldiers to live and fight in their environment, but legionnaires must also be able to survive a ten-day course, described as savage. Many of those in the desert company attend the jungle warfare course in French Guyana and must pass a desert qualification course which takes place in Djibouti. Those selected for maritime operations undergo training off Corsica and learn to operate with small boats, train as frogmen, and be ready to parachute into action with their boats. The amphibious force will, when opportunity arises deploy from a Mistral-class assault ship of the French Navy, allowing teams to exercise the deployment of boats from the warship at night. Urban training revolves around perfecting the skills to mount hostage rescues and adopt evolving tactics for what is called Fighting in Built up Areas (FIBUA). Training takes place with the Gendarmerie Intervention Group at remote camps where 'mock' housing complexes have been built to make training as realistic as a possible.

Training for the specialist skills of demolition, anti-tank teams, sniper, and commando take place across Corsica and Aubagne. As well as French military training areas across France the Commando training often involves cross-training with US forces, as do some of the sniper courses. The regiments use a variety of sniper weapons including the PGM Hécate II, a heavy-calibre rifle. It is described as an anti-materiel rifle and was created in 1995 by the French rifle factory PGM Precision. The Foreign Legion has

The REP often trains and operates with US forces in the Mediterranean region. (Yves Debay/DPL)

been using the design since the late 1990s. It has a 12.7mm calibre, a seven-round magazine, and a range of 7,000 metres. Snipers also use the FR-F2 which has a thermally shielded barrel by means of a polymer shroud. It uses a 7.62mm round, has a ten-round magazine and a range of 800 metres. The FR F2 is being replaced by the SCAR-H PR (Special Operations Forces Combat Assault Rifle), a gas operated, highly accurate semi-auto or selective fire precision rifle for designated marksmen and sniper teams. It was developed by Belgian manufacturer FN Herstal (FN) in the 2000s. In the French Army, it has already replaced the old FR F2. The Legion received first SCAR-H PR rifles in late 2023 but is also retaining its older FR F2s.

The REP has always been the Legion's 'on call' force for operations and since the late 1960s has been constantly deployed. It took part in several campaigns in Chad, the Ivory Coast, Afghanistan, Mali, and Niger. It has also deployed to Djibouti, Lebanon, Rwanda, Gabon, Somalia, Sarajevo, Kosovo, and the Central African Republic.

Terror is nothing new

Now, in the 21st century the REP trains to fight Islamic terrorism - the enemy of western democracies. But fighting fundamentalist terror is not new to the REP. In February 1976, the first terrorist attack by an Islamist group called the Somali Coast Liberation Front (FLCS), took place in Djibouti. Thirty-one foreign children (mostly French) on board a school bus were taken hostage and driven to the frontier with Somalia, where the border guards blocked their passage.

In exchange for the lives of the children, the terrorists demanded that all foreign forces and businesses leave the country, and that all political prisoners be set free. They also demanded that Djibouti should be declared a Fundamental Islamic Republic. When the Republic of Djibouti gained its independence, it had signed a military Memorandum of Understanding (MoU) with France in which Paris trained its army and supported the Djibouti government in extreme situations. The MoU also allowed France to base a limited number of troops withing the new republic and the French Army stationed the 14eme Demi-Brigade of the French Foreign Legion (14ème DBLE) here.

The hijack had started on the morning of February 3, 1976, when a military bus driven

The REP must be able to mount endurance ski marches and are trained to shoot on the move. (Yves Debay/DPL)

The REP train with Middle Eastern forces and have a programme to build partner relations east of Suez. (Bob Morrison/DPL.)

The REP continues to hold flame throwers in their arsenal. (Yves Debay/DPL)

The REP maintains a small number of utility vehicles called the VBL which were last deployed to Kosovo. (Yves Debay/DPL)

While, they are not France's dedicated hostage rescue unit, the Legion train for such situation. (Bob Morrison/DPL)

by 19-year-old soldier Jean-Michel Dupont left the French Air Base within the Ambouli International Airport of Djibouti City. On board with him were 31 children, between five and 12 years old, the sons and daughters of French servicemen serving at the base. At 0715 am the bus was attacked and hijacked by four armed FLCS militants dressed up as women. They ordered the bus driver to go to Loyada, a small village located on the border with Somalia and about 11 miles southeast of Djibouti. At the time, Loyada was the only official border crossing with Somalia.

At around 0745am the bus arrived at the Loyada check-point where the militants were confronted by legionnaires who were on duty at the border post. They were negotiating with the militants when an order arrived from French military command to allow the bus to park in no man's land, between the French and Somali territories, only a few dozen yards from the Somali border outpost.

At the time, elements of the REP were in Djibouti and the remainder of the regiment in Corsica was put on standby to deploy. In the meantime, the company of REP soldiers stationed at the air base left the base for Loyada and in the afternoon, they were reinforced by the Reconnaissance Squadron (ER) of the 13e DBLE, equipped with Panhard AML armoured cars. The 13e DBLE were part of the permanent force in Djibouti and knew the area well. The paratroopers entrenched themselves in a palm grove located around 270 yards from the bus. The REP and 13e DBLE snipers were deployed in an outpost manned by a pro-French police unit consisting of local auxiliaries and French leaders. A second group of REP legionnaires was set next to the outpost and waited.

A team of eight snipers and a commander from the GIGN (the French police special forces unit) arrived in the early morning of February 4 and joined the mission, each equipped with FR F1 rifles. They positioned themselves about 90 yards in front of the REP legionnaires looking directly at the bus while Somali Army troops positioned themselves behind the barbed wire on their side of the border. Their weapons, including machine guns, aimed at French positions. An unspecified number of FLCS militants were also present at the Somali border, some of them later reinforcing the militants aboard the bus during the night.

The French plan was to wait for a moment when all the hijackers were up and visible at the same time so that the GIGN and REP snipers would shoot them dead. At 3.45pm an order was given to rescue the children. As the snipers fired coordinated shots to kill the kidnappers, the Somali guns opened fire on the French. The REP paratroopers launched a frontal attack and ran forward under enemy fire. Lieutenant Doucet's 1st Platoon ran into a grove on the Somali side from which a machine gun was firing. But the lieutenant in the lead was wounded and Staff Sergeant Raoul continued the assault. Right next to them, in the centre, the 2nd Platoon with Staff Sergeant Jorand was running to storm the bus to make sure the children were safe, supported by the Legion snipers of Lieutenant Andrieu. Corporals Larking and Lemoine entered the vehicle and quickly neutralised two militants who had escaped the GIGN fire. Simultaneously, the AML armoured vehicles of the 13e DBLE darted forward to help the REP men neutralise the Somali fire. The GM platoon moved to the GNA outpost to be ready there as a reserve unit and by 4.05 pm the rescue operation was over.

The wheeled mortar has been a long favourite of the Legion. (Yves Debay/DPL)

All the militants aboard the bus were killed as were FLCS militants as well as at least one of the Somali soldiers that had opened fire at legionnaires and French positions. Sadly, a five-year-old girl, Nadine Durand was killed by a gun burst and five children were wounded, two of them seriously. Twenty FLCS militants and Somali troops were wounded in the action. Also, a young boy went missing. It was later discovered that he had been removed from the bus and taken across the border into Somalia. He was named as Franck Rutkovsky, and he was released a few days later.

Lieutenant Doucet, the then commander of 1st Platoon, 2nd Company, REP, was seriously wounded. Valérie Geissbuhler, one of the two seriously injured children was the granddaughter of a former legionnaire. She was flown to hospital in Paris for emergency treatment but died from her injuries a few days later. She was buried in Aubagne - the main garrison town of the Foreign Legion. The other seriously injured child, David Brisson survived but with lasting disability. He committed suicide in 2014.

The 1976 Loyada rescue was the first serious anti-terrorist mission that both the GIGN and the Legion took part in. The wounded were also sent to Paris to be hospitalised. At Camp ➲

The Commando unit of the REP is trained to conduct High Altitude Low Opening (HALO) and High Altitude High Opening (HAHO) jumps. (US DoD)

The REP also trains with the Spanish Legion who routinely training Sardinia. (Yves Debay/DPL)

The amphibious unit is to begin operating with small hand-held drones to track the enemy before the Legion goes ashore. (Yves Debay/DPL)

The REP is being considered for new strike vehicles which can be airlifted by helicopter to the objective. (Bob Morrison/DPL)

Raffalli on April 30, 1976, Lieutenant Doucet and Jehanne Bru, the courageous female assistant, were awarded with the Legion d'Honneur. Five years later, in 1981, Captain Doucet made a full recovery and was posted back to Djibouti, at the head of the 13e DBLE's CECAP Commando training centre. In 2016, the kidnapped children founded an association called The Forgotten of Loyada (Les oubliés de Loyada). They blamed French officials for never being officially recognised as victims of terrorism. In 2019, a French-Belgian film was released titled *15 Minutes of War* (*Intervention* in France), which is said to be inspired by the sad event. The events in Loyada served to generate wider respect for the Legion at home and abroad and highlighted to politicians in France that the Legion was an important part of future plans.

Beirut

In August 1982, the REP was sent to Beirut in the Lebanon tasked to secure the harbour area and establish a bridgehead for the arrival of the main United Nations force. By 11.30pm on August 20, the regiment had secured the harbour and six days later they were given the mission to escort Yasser Arafat and 4,371 Palestinian soldiers out of the region. This was a major contributory factor to peace being restored in the region. The 1990s saw more deployments to Africa and as the 21st century approached; Africa was back on the agenda. An attempted coup d'état in West Africa's Ivory Coast in late 2002 resulted in the Legion's REP being sent on Operation Licorne to maintain order, as well as to protect French and European nationals.

In November, the legionnaires were caught in a firefight at Man airport in the west of the country. A dozen rebels were killed and about 150 foreign nationals were evacuated as the fighting escalated. More soldiers from the REP arrived in the Ivory Coast and on January 6, 2003, 1st Company commanded by Captain Dunant was involved in two battles that took place near the town of Duékoué. A dozen legionnaires were wounded, including one seriously, while about 30 rebels were killed. Shortly afterwards the REP departed. But they were quickly back when the Ivory Coast air force attacked a French military base in the country on November 6, 2004, killing nine soldiers and an American civilian as well as injuring 38 soldiers. The REP was alerted and sent to Ivory Coast, where they secured the airport. The situation was now so volatile that the decision was made to evacuate all French nationals. Reinforcements from the REP arrived and in five days, a total of 5,000 French and foreign nationals were evacuated through the airport allowing the legionnaires to leave. In 2008, while two REP companies were in Gabon and another two were in French Guiana and New Caledonia, the commando element and some HQ men were deployed to join the war in Afghanistan. ●

The use of drones, some as small as your hand is continuously being reviewed by the Legion. (Yves Debay/DPL)

NEW WARS

Legion operations in Afghanistan and Mali

In late 2001, Legionnaires deployed to Kabul, as well as northern and eastern Afghanistan. (DPL)

In the 21st century, the pace of operational commitment has not slowed for the French Foreign Legion. After the attacks on the United States by Osama bin Laden and his cohorts, France was among the first to support the Coalition Task Force created to hunt down the terror networks in Afghanistan. The Legion spent a decade in the country fighting the Taliban as part of the so-called war on terror and then moved into Mali, the former French colony, after a request was made to Paris for assistance amid intelligence fears that more attacks would hit the mainland if France declined to get involved. These new wars have emerged in an era of Islamic terrorism inflicting atrocities across Europe, including the 2015 suicide assaults on Paris, which left 130 civilians dead and more than four hundred injured.

The Legion, like all armies has struggled to adapt to this new asymmetric warfare in which home-made bombs are seeded in areas to shape the fight in a complex and unpredictable environment; and where the enemy uses mobile phone bombs, plants explosives on the backs of dogs and uses children to lure soldiers into traps. In previous deployments the Legion had known their enemy, even in areas such as Bosnia and central Africa where the regiment had been involved in peacekeeping and evacuation missions, the enemy was clear. Today's terrorists and their kin hide among the population and have grasped the weakness of Western politicians who run away from risk when they fear losing public support if their soldiers are being killed.

President Jacques Chirac sent the Legon and other French forces to Afghanistan in late 2001. They operated in Kabul and were ➲

In 2008, the Legion deployed VAB personnel carriers to Sirobi in Afghanistan's Kapisa Province. (DPL)

In Afghanistan, the Legion faced multiple asymmetric threats from al-Qaeda terrorists. (DPL)

in the forefront of operations tasked to drive the Taliban from Kabul, destroy Al Qaeda's training camps, and help set up a training regime to develop the Afghan National Army. On November 15, the French deployed a contingent of special forces to the mountains of Tora Bora to support the hunt for bin Laden and later moved to the Mazar-i-Sharif region before being redeployed to Kabul airport. These forces mounted a surveillance mission around the capital and its northern approaches to secure the airport and the command headquarters. Then at the NATO summit in Riga, in 2008, France agreed to deploy troops to eastern Afghanistan in Kapisa Province. In August 2008, a French task force had just replaced an Italian contingent in the west of the country when a convoy of French troops including soldiers from the 8th Marine Infantry Parachute Regiment (RIMa) and 2nd Foreign Parachute Regiment was ambushed in the Uzbin.

The Taliban attacked in force killing nine soldiers and wounding 21. It had been alleged that the Italians were paying bribes to the

During the conflicts in Afghanistan, the Legion relied on Coalition forces for helicopter support. (US DoD)

In August 2008, the Legion deployed soldiers into Kabul. (DPL)

insurgents to stop attacks in the area and Taliban commander, Mohammed Ismayel confirmed the existence of a deal with the Italians. He declined to corroborate the existence of any financial transactions, but he claimed the French Foreign Legion had a more aggressive attitude and had caused the Taliban to attack. The Italian leader Silvio Berlusconi denied that any bribes were ever paid and rejected the claims as 'totally baseless accusations'. The losses were the heaviest suffered by the French military since the 1983 Beirut barracks bombings and the attack shocked the public - prompting calls for France to pull out of Afghanistan. Instead, the government accelerated the deployment of critical equipment requested by the military.

Withdrawals

In January 2012, after an Afghan soldier working with the French shot and killed four French soldiers in eastern Afghanistan, French President Nicolas Sarkozy threatened to suspend French operations in Afghanistan. Five months later the newly elected President Francois Hollande announced that he would be withdrawing 2,000 of France's 3,400 troops from Afghanistan, leaving 1,400 in country for training and logistics. By November the withdrawal had happened. Many of the Legion's units had served three or four tours in Afghanistan, with legionnaires often claiming it was a political war. Andre Garnier, who

A Legion sniper team in Afghanistan. (FFL)

The Malian terrain encountered during Operation Serval was open desert with little vegetation for cover and only isolated hamlets. (French Armed Forces)

served with the Legion in Afghanistan said it was a war of political correctness, he added: "Every week NATO was reminding us that we could not use lethal force unless we could see an insurgent with a weapon that actually threatened us. These people had no idea, by the time he points his weapon at you it is too late. Our hands were tied, the politicians wanted us to be there to keep the allies happy, but they did not want us getting involved in fighting and perhaps killed, that would cause them to lose public support. They sent the wrong people; we are the Legion."

Mali

France's relationship with Africa, and particularly the French Foreign Legion, is closely linked to its colonial past. Mali gained

In 2013, the Legion moved into Mali where an offensive and a UN mission operated side by side. (United Nations)

its independence in 1960 and has since maintained a close relationship with its former imperial overlords in Paris, based around economic support and military training. Formerly known as French Sudan, in which officials ruled from the capital in Bamako, Mali called on France for help with its fights against rebel fighters in 2013. Paris agreed to send a limited force, with the political rationale being that choosing not to help Mali would allow a terrorist state to develop on the doorstep of France and Europe.

At the time, Islamic attacks in France were increasing. In 2012 the country recorded 65 incidents in which seven people were killed and the government promoted the Mali deployment to the public as being a responsible measure to protect the mainland. ➲

January 2013 and the first legionnaires are flown out to Mali for what was named Operation Serval. (FFL)

The Malian rebels were armed but their most effective 'weapon' was their knowledge of the terrain and the weather. (French Armed Forces)

During the Malian operations, the Legion was supported by RAF Chinook helicopters for casualty evacuation. (FFL)

The Malian rebel attacks increased against the French with IEDs, rocket propelled grenades and attempts to shoot down helicopters. (French Armed Forces)

On January 28, 2013, a 200 strong assault force, drawn from the REP, assembled at an airfield just outside of the city of Abidjan in readiness to mount a night jump into Mali. (FFL)

On January 28, 2013, a 200 strong assault force, drawn from the REP, assembled at an airfield just outside the city of Abidjan, in the Ivory Coast under the umbrella story to the west African government that they were mounting a training jump. After a briefing, the paratroopers boarded three C-160s and two C-130s and took off in readiness for a night jump into northern Mali. Among those who jumped was Staff Sergeant Harold Vormezeele who was born on July 24, 1979, in Belgium.

Staff Sgt Vormezeele

He joined the Foreign Legion as a volunteer at the age of just 19 and signed a five-year contract of service. At the end of his four-month basic training in the 4th Foreign Regiment at Castelnaudary, he asked to join the REP which he joined in late July 1999. In August 2000, he became a radio operator. Noted by his commanders as a serious and motivated legionnaire, he was quickly promoted

In early January 2013, a force of 1,700 soldiers started to arrive in Mali and the force included the 1st Foreign Cavalry Regiment who took part in initial operations to recapture the town of Diabaly, which had been seized by Islamic extremists. The regiment deployed with its AMX 10 armoured vehicles to provide mobile artillery support to the wider French force.

Many legionnaires regarded modern day interventions in Africa as nothing more than peacekeeping missions, but Mali offered the prospect of offensive direct action against militants whose ideology had killed French citizens. An initial task for the regiment was to stop Tuareg fighters who were mounting hit and run attacks from the north of the country. Commanders planned to cut their escape route into the northern desert and mountains by dropping paratroopers from the French Foreign Legion north of Timbuktu. The aim was to deny the Isamists an exit and allow the Malian army to deal with them.

After a briefing, the paratroopers boarded three C-160s and two C-130s and mounted for a night jump north of Timbuktu. The date, January 28, 2013. (French Armed Forces)

The town of Timbuktu offered sanctuary to the rebel fighters and Operation Serval was intended to force them out. (FFL)

Among those who jumped in Operation Serval was Staff Sergeant Harold Vormezeele who was killed in a fire-fight with the enemy. (FFL)

to corporal in 2002 and just three years later made the rank of sergeant. Sgt Vormezeele joined the parachute commando group (GCP) and was award French citizenship having completed his contract. Having signed on again he was a made staff sergeant in 2013 and had now gained immense operational experience serving in Bosnia-Herzegovina (former Yugoslavia), Gabon in Djibouti, New Caledonia, Ivory Coast, the Central African Republic in 2007, and Afghanistan in 2008, 2010 and 2011. On January 23, 2013, he was sent again to Ivory Coast in Africa and during the night of January 27 to 28, he was among REP force which jumped into Mali, as part of Operation Serval. Several weeks later his company was still engaging Tuareg fighters in the Adrar des Ifoghas massif of northern Mali – a mountainous area which the rebels knew well. Skirmishes with the rebels were constant and on February 19, Staff Sergeant Vormezeele was killed during an assault against a Tuareg position. His team killed more than 20 rebels. Sgt Vormezeele became the second French soldier to be killed during Operation Serval in Mali. He was awarded the Military Valour Cross and was posthumously promoted to adjutant. He is buried in Paris.

In 2014 France expanded its operations as violence spread to Burkina Faso and Niger. Paris increased its force strength to 5,100 troops who were deployed across the Sahel countries of Burkina Faso, Chad, Niger, and Mali. Operation Serval was now replaced with a new mission, codenamed Operation Barkhane. Between May and June 2015, the Malian government and former Tuareg rebels signed a peace agreement, but it was never fully implemented and failed to achieve a cease-fire or any further negotiations. By autumn of 2018 the fighting continued, and the Legion was using parachute assaults to outmanoeuvre the rebels or cut-off their planned offensives. On September 27, more than 100 soldiers from ➲

On September 27, 2018, the REP mounted another jump into the Menaka region of northern Mali. (FFL)

In November 2019 two helicopters crashed in Mali killing 19 French soldiers - among them Legion Staff Sergeant Andreï Jouk. (FFL)

with the loss of 13 soldiers, including a French Foreign legionnaire from the 2nd Foreign Engineer Regiment. He was Staff Sergeant Andreï Jouk.

Andreï had joined the Legion at 32, in January 2008. After the four-month basic training in Castelnaudary, he was assigned to the 2e REG, and promoted to corporal in 2010 and to sergeant in 2011. During his 11 years in the Legion, Ssgt Jouk served in Afghanistan, in Djibouti, in French Guiana, and completed three tours in Mali. Having been promoted to staff sergeant in January 2018, he had been selected for the prestigious Mountain Commando Group.

In August 2020, a coup led by Colonel Assimi Goita grabbed power in Mali. Goita carried out a second coup by dismissing the civilian leaders in Mali's transitional government and putting himself in charge last year. More instability followed when Mali's transitional government allowed Russian mercenaries from the Wagner Group to deploy

the REP conducted an airborne operation in the Ménaka region of northeastern Mali near the Niger border. The REP commando force dropped from an Airbus A400M Atlas. It was their first operational drop from the new aircraft and the team exited by the rear ramp, using the High Altitude Low Opening (HALO) technique which involves the parachutist opening his canopy at a low altitude after free-falling for a period of time. On the ground two units of Malian armed forces linked up with the paratroopers who formed the spearhead element of the Desert Battle Group which had been established within Operation Barkhane.

At the time the French armed forces spokesperson Colonel Patrik Steiger said: "We combine different capabilities to create a surprise effect among armed terrorist groups and to show the population that we are able to come quickly [to their aid]."

On November 25 of the following year, two helicopters of the French Army crashed in Mali

Operation Barkhane came under threat as the Malian administration faced a coup. (FFL)

The Malian government had agreed a deal with the Tuareg rebels which quickly collapsed, and they then turned to Russian for help. (French Armed Forces)

In 2022 President Emmanuel Macron announced the complete withdrawal of troops from Mali. (Elysée Palace)

on its territory. The Private Military Contractor (PMC) arrived in Mali in late December 2021 after Moscow offered to support Goita. It was alleged at the time that Putin saw Mali as an opportunity to secure a foothold of military influence in Africa.

The Russian move into Africa came after the political relationship with Paris deteriorated rapidly when the Mali administration refused to hold an election. Later, in June 2021, President Emmanuel Macron announced that the French military presence was being reduced to 2,500 men. This may have been the catalyst for Goita to approach Russia – fearing that without French support he would risk being ousted from power himself. Just a year later thousands of anti French protestors take to the streets waving Russian flags and burning cardboard cut-outs of the French President. Ten days later Macron announced the total withdrawal of troops from Mali. Rising violence was not the only factor that contributed to the termination of the French operation in Mali. Macron's announcement explicitly named the primary reason for France's withdrawal as the junta's unwillingness to solve its own security issues and the hiring of Russian mercenaries. France had become increasingly unpopular throughout the Sahel, where indigenous people blamed Paris for the lack of economic development and what was seen as 'colonial control'- although it was the Malian government who had requested the French intervention.

The Legion Legacy

In the 21st century the Legion continues to fight for France - a role it has carried out since 1831. The force is composed of foreigners whose characteristics and qualities are now globally known and recognised. While it was initially created for the role of guarding the French colonial empire, the Foreign Legion has continued to fight for Paris and its regimental standard bears the names of the most glorious battles in the history of France. Each volunteer continues to sign a pact with the Republic and despite France not being their native country, foreign volunteers take the oath to be ready to give their life for it.

The Legion consists of more than 9,000 soldiers who all accept that French is more than just a working or official language. It is the vector of integration that brings foreigners, who have deliberately chosen to serve France, together. Discipline, respect and solidarity are the cardinal values cultivated by the legionnaires in a modern force integrated with the regular French Army.

The Legion is Immensely proud of its traditions, the white kepi worn with a khaki-colour cover in Algeria and Morocco is seen as the instant hallmark of the force. On July 14, 1939, in Paris, the white kepis were officially used by legionnaires on parade for the first time. A kepi with the white cover was listed as a prescribed cap for the Legion in 1959. However, a khaki cover for kepi and was still used during instruction until the 1970s. Today, legionnaires use only white kepis. The traditional shoulder pads appeared for the first time in 1868 and have been integrated to the ceremonial parade dress uniform since 1946. The Legion uses epaulettes in green and red which are its official colours.

The Legion regularly trains with US forces. (US DoD)

The Legion is a regiment for life and since formation, it has always cared for its own wounded. In Algeria, rest centres were established to accommodate its sick and wounded soldiers of the various French overseas military campaigns. In 1934, General Rollet created the House of the Legionnaires in Auriol. Then in 1954, the Foreign Legion acquired the Danjou's Domain, in Puyloubier, and installed there the Institution for Invalids of the Foreign Legion to cure the wounded from Indochina and Algeria. More recently in 2010, in the same spirit of solidarity and gratitude, the Legion decided to establish 'a day of the wounded' in all Legion regiments.

For decades French politicians, like many elected to office reflect the vision of Rudyard Kipling's poem 'Tommy' and have been quick to call on the Legion in time of conflict and then forget them when the war is over. The Legion is perhaps one of the most cost-effective regiments of the French Army. It has overcome numerous scandals about its operations spanning from the coup in Algeria, after which de Gaulle would have been happy to see the force disbanded, to allegations of extreme bullying which the Legion found hard to defend. In an uncertain and unstable world, the future for the Legion will continue as long as politicians have a stomach for war.

There seems to be a never- ending supply of young men seeking adventure and action in the ranks of the Legion. But as France steps back from its policy of military intervention there are fears that the country will adopt a more isolationist posture and avoid the expensive wars in areas such as Afghanistan.

The French parliament has approved a future defence budget, until 2030 of $450 billion. Much of this is assigned to a new aircraft carrier, new warships, fighter jets and missile systems – with little allocated to the army. The Legion's cavalry is expected to receive the new Jaguar reconnaissance vehicle as a replacement for the AMX-10RC while the infantry anticipates a new advanced anti-tank weapon. The REP, the parachute regiment, are due a replacement canopy for its current static line parachutes.

Liam Campbell who served with the Legion for ten years said the Legion is never top of the list when it comes to the delivery of new equipment, he added: "There are some in the political establishment who have no time for the Legion, but they know that the public love us. When I was in the regiment, we never expected to get any new equipment. We just soldiered on with what we had and made it work. At the end of the day, the Legion represents France but fights for the regiment. As always, we may see some cutbacks but as we always say, 'the Legion will never die'".

A senior French Foreign Legion officer giving a presentation to British soldiers said that the Legion does not worry about politicians and the potential that the Legion may become un-fashionable. He said: "For the Legionnaire, death is not the enemy, but a close and constant companion who will one day call the Legionnaire to lay down his arms and rest."

In 2024 and looking ahead to 2025 the legion retains a high-profile role in the internal security operation to protect Paris and mainland France. (FFL)

The Legion is to be equipped with a new Armoured Reconnaissance and Combat Vehicle called the Jaguar that will replace the AMX-10. (French MoD)